Teaching and Training Vocational Learners

Teaching and Training Vocational Learners

Steve Ingle and Vicky Duckworth

Los Angeles | London | New Delhi
Singapore | Washington DC

Learning Matters
An imprint of SAGE Publications Ltd
1 Oliver's Yard
55 City Road
London EC1Y 1SP

SAGE Publications Inc.
2455 Teller Road
Thousand Oaks, California 91320

SAGE Publications India Pvt Ltd 150
B 1/1 1 Mohan Cooperative Industrial Area
Mathura Road
New Delhi 110 044

SAGE Publications Asia-Pacific Pte Ltd
3 Church Street
#10–04 Samsung Hub
Singapore 049483

Editor: Amy Thornton
Development editor: Jennifer Clark
Production controller: Chris Marke
Project management: Deer Park Productions, Tavistock, Devon, England
Marketing manager: Catherine Slinn
Cover design: Wendy Scott
Typeset by: C&M Digitals (P) Ltd, Chennai, India
Printed in Great Britain by Henry Ling Limited at the Dorset Press, Dorchester, DT1 1HD

Library of Congress Control Number: 2013947934

British Library Cataloguing in Publication Data

A catalogue record for this book is available from the British Library.

MIX
Paper from
responsible sources
FSC
www.fsc.org
FSC™ C013985

ISBN: 978-1-4462-7438-5
ISBN: 978-1-4462-7439-2 (pbk)

Steve and Vicky would like to dedicate this book to all those involved with changing lives and improving futures through high quality, inspirational vocational education and training.

Steve would like to dedicate this book to his mum Gwen, a true lifelong learner.

Vicky would like to dedicate this book, as always, to Craig Ludlow and their daughters Anna and Niamh.

CONTENTS

About the authors   viii
Acknowledgements   ix

Introduction   xi

1   What is vocational education?   1

2   The changing landscape   24

3   Engaging and motivating vocational learners   41

4   Employer engagement   59

5   Planning your approach   74

6   Experiential and applied learning   103

7   Vocational assessment   125

8   Observing vocational learning   141

9   The practitioner voice   151

Appendix 1: Example of a vocational scheme of work   165
Appendix 2: Assessment plan template   179
Appendix 3: IRIS reflection template   180
Index   181

ABOUT THE AUTHORS

Steve Ingle is a freelance consultant and Chief Examiner and Associate Lecturer at the University of Cumbria, UK. He has over twelve years' experience with Grade 1 providers across the Further Education and Skills Sector, holding a variety of teaching and management positions within further and higher education, sixth form and private training providers.

An experienced teacher educator, Steve has worked on a range of quality improvement and workforce development programmes for national providers. A specialist in vocational education and technology enhanced learning, Steve has significant experience of external assessment and quality assurance. He holds fellowships with the CIEA, IfL and HE Academy. For more information on his work, please go to www.steveingle.com.

Vicky Duckworth is Senior Lecturer and MA co-ordinator for Post-Compulsory Education and Training and Schools' University Lead at Edge Hill University, UK.

Vicky has a passionate belief that further education can offer a critical space to support and empower learners, no matter what their trajectory so far. She has published several works on a range of issues and research topics. These topics vary from critical and emancipatory approaches to education, to further education teaching to social justice, literacies and community engagement.

ACKNOWLEDGEMENTS

The authors wish to extend their most grateful thanks to all those who have contributed their time, ideas and inspiration in shaping this text for the benefit of other practitioners.

In particular, thanks go to Hannah Ratcliffe, David Knowles, Elizabeth Bennett, Erica Campbell, Samantha Watters, Deborah Parkinson, Clare Stuart, Debra Manley, Abigail Heaton, Naomi Wilson, Claire Elliott and all current practitioners who have illustrated their innovative use of learning technologies:

Alan Goodenough – Blackburn College

John Picken – Blackburn College University Centre

Julie Gibson – SportsED

Beth Maloney and Simon Coel – Horses and Courses

Penny Horsefield – International School of Creative Arts

Rani Padayachee – Lambeth College

Sandra Arnold-Jenkins – Lambeth College

Jenny Stimpson – Fresh Media Productions

Helen Green – Orient8 Consulting

Lenny St Jean – Play with Jelly

Catherine Shiel – West Lancashire College

Thanks must also go to Amy Thornton at Learning Matters and Jennifer Clark for their patient support and guidance.

The structure of the book and how to use it

Welcome to *Teaching and Training Vocational Learners*. This book provides an accessible and user-friendly guide for new teachers and tutors in training and for more experienced colleagues teaching vocational learners across the diverse breadth of the FE and Skills sector, including further education and sixth-form colleges, adult and community learning, work-based learning, private training providers and those working in prison education.

This book aims to:

- familiarise you and keep you updated with the changing landscape of vocational education in the UK;

- provide you with practical ideas, tips, activities and plans to support and enhance your teaching and training;

- help you learn from other vocational practitioners by exploring what they are doing in their own practice, in their own diverse learning settings;

- hear from the 'vocational learner voice' and hear how vocational learners view their education and what they want from their tutors.

The vocational education and training (VET) landscape has seen much attention and change over recent times. Whilst this is an interesting time for vocational education practitioners and learners, recent changes and debates can be confusing and unsettling, particularly for those currently in training or those colleagues new to vocational teaching or the vocational educator sector. Changes influenced by: the impact of the Wolf Review of vocational education; the Lingfield Review of professionalism in further education; the Richard Review of apprenticeships; the opening of University Technical Colleges (UTCs) and studio schools; the re-design of BTEC qualifications to include external assessment; are just a few of the recent indicators of the current debate, shift and thinking around the future and value of vocational education in the UK.

We hope that this book provides a comprehensible and accessible text to support all practitioners to navigate their way around and deliver excellent workplace and college learning. It has been designed to offer practical advice and guidance to help shape your approach to teaching, learning and assessment. We use the terms 'practitioner' and 'tutor' interchangeably to indicate anyone working across this diverse sector – for example, teachers, tutors, trainers, lecturers, support workers, facilitators, mentors and coaches. This could include supporting your practice in the salon, the workshop, the kitchen, on the pitch, in the garden, in the water, the classroom or the lecture theatre.

Each chapter offers very practical information, advice and guidance to support your work as a dual professional: both as an industry expert and a developing practitioner. We recognise that many years of experience and expertise in the workplace do not always prepare you to 'CHIME' with your learners straight away:

- **C**ommunicate;

- **H**elp;

- **I**nspire;

- **M**otivate;

- **E**ngage.

Chapter 1 aims to investigate what vocational education and training actually is, the differences from more general education and general qualifications and how this might influence your approach to teaching, learning and assessment design and practice. We draw on the work of Professors Bill Lucas, Guy Claxton and Dr Ellen Spencer and their thoughts and recommendations for a 'vocational pedagogy' – the science, art and craft of teaching. We also explore the work of the Commission for Adult Vocational Teaching and Learning and the recommendations it offers practitioners in enabling excellent teaching and learning.

Chapter 2 explores some of the current debates around vocational education and training in the UK. The pace of change is challenging and often daunting. The excellent vocational practitioner is charged with keeping up to date with current debates and how these influence policy and ultimately practice. As we write, many changes are on-going and we signpost readers to sources of further support and advice in order to stay informed.

Chapter 3 highlights the importance of engaging and motivating vocational learners. We explore case studies from existing and experienced practitioners and how their approach might help guide and shape your practice.

Employer engagement is a key factor in offering effective vocational learning experiences that prepare learners to develop the knowledge, understanding and skills required for the real world of work. Chapter 4 explores how practitioners might work with employers and the industry to ensure teaching, learning and assessment are closely aligned to the needs of employers.

Planning your approach to vocational teaching and training is often one of the most challenging aspects for new teachers, tutors and trainers. Getting the planning right should help to ensure that delivery and assessment are also highly effective. In Chapter 5, we offer a range of ideas and strategies, including examples of lesson plans and schemes of work, to help guide and support you through the planning of your own vocational course, qualifications and programmes.

Chapter 6 moves on to explore ways to make your vocational practice experiential, active and participatory. Practitioners share examples of how their teaching meets the needs of vocational learners through the use of a range of engaging and motivational activities, trips, visits, tasks, guest speakers and challenges. We unpack the role of learning technologies in vocational education and how simulations and 'serious games' can provide valuable vocational learning experiences.

In Chapter 7, we explore the multi-modal and multimedia approach to vocational learning assessment and feedback. Vocational learning is demonstrated in many different ways, in a huge variety of contexts. The need to take flexible approaches to both formative (on-going) and summative (final) assessment is highlighted, including the use of presentations, portfolios, role-plays and scenarios and work-place evidence. We present ideas for producing vocationally relevant and engaging assignment briefs, with useful examples.

Vocational education often produces a large amount of assessment evidence, which demonstrates learners' knowledge, understanding and skills, in both the process and final product stage. Much of this assessment is focused on confirming skills competence and the knowledge and understanding learners have to complete vocational tasks and activities. Chapter 8 explores the use of electronic portfolios (and more commonly e-Portfolios) as well as other new and emerging technologies that can be used to record evidence. We also explore how to observe learners' applied skills and record the evidence appropriately to stand up to both internal and external quality assurance. We highlight the differences between evidence confirmed by the assessor and the use of expert or witness testimonies and the ways to capture robust evidence.

The final chapter is given to a range of diverse 'learner voices' from across the FE and Skills sector. It draws together and illustrates the needs and motivations of a wide spectrum of vocational learners across different ages, disciplines and backgrounds. We pose questions and areas for professional reflection at this time of exciting but considerable change for all those working to plan, deliver and evaluate outstanding vocational education and training for young people and adults. We offer a new model for reflective practice to support you in planning your next steps, how you will be supported and what changes you wish to take forward in your developing practice.

Within each chapter, you are invited to reflect, pause and participate in a series of tasks and extension activities. These are useful to apply your developing knowledge and understanding to your own practice and professional context.

Case studies – these help to illustrate what other practitioners are doing across the diverse FE and Skills training sector. Consider if aspects of their practice would work for you, the challenges they have faced and the recommendations they suggest for engaging and developing vocational learners.

Reflection points – to prompt on-going personal reflection and a deeper understanding of the topics introduced. Reflective practice is viewed as an essential quality of teaching and learning professionals, in order to help you critically engage with the current issues and to identify practical actions and targets for future practice.

Extension activities – suggestions to consolidate and apply learning to your own practice. Activities may be challenging depending on your current level of experience. We invite you to find out more about your current professional contexts and the needs and preferences of your vocational learners.

Theory focus and websites – understanding why we teach and train in the way that we do is important to inform and guide our professional development. The vocational landscape is ever changing and we signpost links to relevant research and sources of current information.

Each chapter is also linked to the National Occupational Standards (NOS) for learning and development units. The standards were first approved in 2001, by Lifelong Learning UK (LLUK), which was the Sector Skills Council (SSC) for the learning sector, and updated in 2010.

National Occupational Standards (NOS) are those standards that describe what a person needs to do, know and understand in their job, in order to carry out their role in a consistent and competent way. The Standards have been used by a range of learning and development practitioners in developing and assessing the skills, knowledge and competence of learners in the workplace or in work-related programmes of learning.

Links to these Standards may be particularly useful for those working towards a qualification in Training Assessment Quality Assurance (TAQA). The TAQA units and qualifications support and develop the practice of assessors and those involved with internal quality assurance (such as internal verifiers and moderators) on both accredited and non-accredited learning programmes.

There are 13 NOS for Learning and Development, which are based on a 'training or learning cycle'.

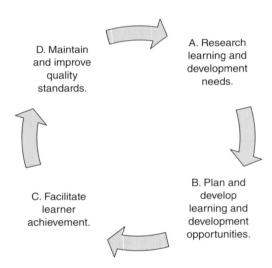

Figure 0.1   Training and learning cycle

Other national occupational standards that might be relevant to your role include:

Engaging employers – for all individuals who are employed by a FE and Skills organisation who work directly with the employer/employers.

Learning delivery – for those practitioners involved with the design, development and delivery of learning.

Personal tutoring – for those working in a personal tutoring role, supporting wider needs and removing barriers of vocational students.

Supporting teaching and learning – for those who support teachers and tutors in providing learning activities, for example learning support assistants (LSAs), teaching assistants (TAs) and learning mentors.

To find out more about national occupational standards and those that guide and support those working in your professional sector, visit the dedicated website from the Commission for UK Employment and Skills (UKCES): http://nos.ukces.org.uk

Above all, this book is designed with you in mind: the busy vocational practitioner. Dip into chapters, find specific tools and examples, and link to relevant theory and further information. We hope you find it a useful resource in supporting your practice in delivering outstanding teaching, learning and assessment, which meets the needs of all your vocational learners.

Steve Ingle and Vicky Duckworth

October 2013

1 WHAT IS VOCATIONAL EDUCATION?

In this chapter you will learn about:

- the complex nature of vocational education and training;
- the similarities and differences between general 'academic' and vocational qualifications;
- the range of vocational qualifications and contexts across the further education and training sector;
- ideas for developing a vocational pedagogy or andragogy for effective teaching and training of vocational adults and young people.

Professional Standards

Standard 10: Reflect on, develop and maintain own skills and practice in learning and development – KU15 How research can help to update practice

Standard 13: Evaluate and improve learning and development provision – KU3 How to research and keep up to date with quality requirements relevant to learning and development

Introduction

Vocation, profession or trade?

When first entering the world of 'vocational education', the specific terminology and sheer range of qualifications can be very confusing and daunting for the beginning practitioner or tutor. This chapter explores the changing view of vocational education or, as it is sometimes known, vocational education and training (VET). It also outlines how this view translates to the range of qualifications delivered and assessed by practitioners across the country, whether in further education or sixth-form colleges, adult and community learning venues, with offenders in prison environments or in the large workplace learning sector.

By developing an understanding of the debates around vocational education, you will be better placed to develop and design vocational courses, programmes and assessments that meet the needs and interests of your learners, in school, colleges and in the workplace.

Activity

What does the term 'vocational education' mean to you? Consider your own educational background and the different routes that have brought you towards becoming an educator of others. Make a list of the terms.

When considering the term 'vocational education', you may have come up with a list of terms such as:

- technical and hands-on;
- occupationally focused;
- practical and applied learning;
- skills development for the real world of work;
- work-related and work-based competence.

So what is vocational education? Tummons (2007: 3) highlights how the language around vocational education has shifted and is sometimes unclear.

> *Historically, some occupations have been classed as professions and others as vocations. The word vocation derives from the Latin word, vocare, which means 'to call'. Originally, professions were seen as being distinct from vocations, and from other occupations.*

Today, we often talk of the teaching, medical and legal professions, but could these not also be considered as vocations, where practitioners have some sense of calling to do the role? In her review of vocational education in England, Professor Alison Wolf (2011) also identified how in the absence of a formal definition, the term 'vocational' is not clearly defined by the education community. Vocational education, and its associated range of qualifications, serves many different purposes and many different learners, from high-level courses geared toward very specific occupations to more general, work-related or pre-vocational programmes, often offered at the lower levels.

In a report on excellent adult vocational teaching and learning, the Commission on Adult Vocational Teaching and Learning (CAVTL, 2013) recognises the tricky and fluid nature of defining the term 'vocational' and its distinction from 'professional' and traditionally 'academic' education. They identify how vocational education and training has traditionally been associated with the development of skills for the craft and trade industries, such as catering, plumbing, joinery and hairdressing at around an intermediate level. Professional education could be more closely associated with medicine, law and accountancy at a higher level and there are, of course, other occupational areas which appear to sit somewhere in between, such as business, engineering and information technology.

CAVTL identifies that any vocational teaching and learning programme must be characterised by two defining factors:

1. a **'clear line of sight to work'** – to enable learners to see why the what they are learning for the real world of work;

2. a **'two-way street'** collaboration – between training providers and employers.

Reflection point

Consider the subject that you teach. Do you view your subject as vocational, academic, general or professional?

Do you think the level at which you teach your subject has an impact on whether it is vocational or not?

The Edge Foundation is an independent education charity dedicated to raising the status of technical, practical and vocational learning. The Foundation offers a definition of vocational education where learning is demonstrated through the application of knowledge in a practical context. This places an emphasis on 'learning by doing', where clear links are made between theory and practice, as opposed to the more theoretical and abstract learning seen in non-vocational or more 'academic' education.

Extension Activity

The Edge Foundation (www.edge.co.uk)

The Edge Foundation is an independent education charity dedicated to raising the status of technical, practical and vocational learning. Edge believes that all young people should have the opportunity to achieve their potential. This potential can be achieved through a number of different paths, whether by following a predominantly academic or a 'learning by doing' vocational route. Vocational skills are seen as crucial in equipping the UK's future workforce to be successful in a modern, global economy.

Edge believes that the current system places a disproportionate value on academic education and this needs to change. Its campaigning, networking and research is aimed at creating a more equal status for technical, practical and vocational education, which should be an integral part of education in order to meet the demands of the UK economy.

Investigate the role of Edge and the resources that may be useful to you in your role as a vocational educator.

Education or training?

When considering the debate around vocational education, the role of training is also a key area of focus. When does education become training, or vice-versa? Training is often

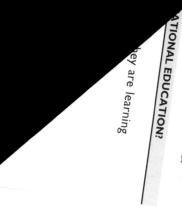

to have the procedural knowledge, or 'know-how', in order to
ar skill or procedure. This specific knowledge is often seen as
)n term often used to describe vocational programmes.

/iewed as developing an understanding of more theoretical or
referred to as declarative or propositional knowledge, or the
many vocational programmes seek to develop both declarative
Jge, so that learners don't just know how to perform a task or
why, and crucially, the consequences of getting it wrong.

Activity

Consider your own subject and the different types of knowledge that your own teaching is designed to develop. Is it mainly procedural, for example how to wire a plug or change a tyre, or propositional, such as a theory of child development or the impact of contraindications in beauty therapy?

Now consider the ways that might be the most effective in developing your learning knowledge of both procedural and propositional knowledge. Would you use different methods and activities? Would you assess the different types of knowledge in different ways?

We will explore these issues further in subsequent chapters.

Academic or vocational?

In today's teaching and learning landscape, both in schools and throughout the FE and Skills sector, a clear distinction is often made between the 'academic' and the 'vocational' curriculum, although in reality, there are many academic aspects in many vocational programmes. General qualifications, such as GCSEs and A levels, are often viewed as an academic curriculum, preparing learners to have an understanding of facts, figures, theories and concepts – propositional knowledge.

The role of the vocational curriculum, and the many associated qualifications such as BTECs, OCR Nationals, National Vocational Qualifications (NVQs) and Vocationally Related Qualification (VRQs), is seen by many as a way to develop learners' procedural knowledge, the practical skills required to carry out many manual and skilled roles.

In the UK, general 'academic' qualifications are often seen as more demanding and challenging and therefore a curriculum more suited to the most able and gifted learners. However, many vocational qualifications include rigorous and challenging academic and theoretical concepts, alongside the development of highly technical, practical skills. Despite high status in other developed nations, such as Germany and the Netherlands, the perceived disparity between the academic and vocational curricula in England has a significant history. This debate continues, along with a range of interventions designed to address and close the 'gap' and raise the status of technical and vocational education in England, such as the introduction of University Technical Colleges (UTCs), which are explored further in Chapter 2.

Reflection point

Commissioned by the Edge Foundation for the Baker Dearing Educational Trust, Richardson and Wiborg (2010) completed a report reviewing trends in technical and vocational education since the 1880s in the UK and four other countries: Germany, the USA, Japan and Sweden.

Reflect on and consider the report summary and your own feelings in relation to the current view of vocational education in the UK compared with other nations. What changes would you like to make and how might these be achieved?

Available from www.edge.co.uk/media/1699/considerations_for_university_technical_colleges.pdf

So although there are some difficulties in reaching a single formal definition, a number of common factors which are key to vocational education are:

- the development of knowledge, understanding and skills related to a broad or more specific vocational context or sector;

- an occupationally focused curriculum that requires practical application of knowledge and understanding;

- education and training which prepares students to apply their learning to work-based contexts.

Extension Activity

In 2011, Professor Alison Wolf was asked to review vocational education in England and to investigate to what extent it provides for progression to higher learning and employment.

The report outlines a number of key facts:

- *Around 2.5 million young people in England are aged 14 to 19, the vast majority of whom are engaged in full- or part-time education.*

- *Most English young people now take some vocational courses before they are 16; and post-16 the majority follow courses that are largely or entirely vocational.*

- *Vocational education includes courses and programmes which teach important and valuable skills to a very high standard. It offers a direct route into higher education.*

- *Many 16- and 17-year-olds move in and out of education and short-term employment.*

(Continued)

(Continued)

- *Between a quarter and a third of the post-16 cohort take low-level vocational qualifications, most of which have little to no labour market value.*

- *Among 16- to 19-year-olds, the review estimates that at least 350,000 get little to no benefit from the post-16 education system.*

- *Under 50 per cent of students have both English and Maths GCSE (at grades A*–C) at the end of Key Stage 4 (age 15/16); and at age 18 the figure is still below 50 per cent. Only 4 per cent of the cohort achieves this during their 16–18 education.*

- *Many of England's 14–19-year-olds do not progress successfully into either secure employment or higher-level education and training, with many leaving education without the skills that will enable them to progress at a later date.*

The Wolf Report made a number of significant recommendations in order to reform the face of vocational education in England. The recommendations affect many teaching professionals working in the FE and Skills sector today.

Consider the recommendations made in the Wolf Report and how these affect your daily role as a practitioner or tutor.

Vocational qualifications

One of the Wolf Report's recommendations was to review the high number of vocational qualifications available and how these are accredited. For the FE and Skills tutor, the range and number of qualifications can be overwhelming at first, each with their unique structure, delivery guidance and assessment framework.

Activity

Consider your own institution and the range of qualifications on offer. List all the different qualification titles, levels and awarding organisations involved. Identify the key features and differences.

Depending on which type of organisation in the sector you currently work in, your list of qualifications is likely to be quite comprehensive, particularly in work-based learning. If you are teaching accredited learning, your list might including Apprenticeships, BTECs, NVQs, VRQs, Applied A levels or GCSEs, Foundation Learning and Functional Skills, to name but a few! Some learning providers also offer non-accredited provision: those programmes that do not lead to a nationally recognised qualification. A process of recognising and recording progress and achievement (RARPA) can be used by many organisations offering non-accredited learning, for example some charities, local authorities and community groups. Further information on using the RARPA framework to plan vocational learning is explored in Chapter 5.

Changes to accredited qualifications are frequent in the FE and Skills sector and it is often very difficult to maintain a good working knowledge of the latest developments and the impact of government policy. Keeping up with the changes is essential however, as you are very likely to be working within a qualification-driven setting, linked to public funding.

Most publicly funded qualifications are accredited to either the Qualifications and Credit Framework (QCF) or the National Qualifications Framework (NQF), both of which are regulated by the Office for Qualifications and Examinations Regulation (Ofqual).

Qualifications on the QCF are made up of units, each with a credit value depending on its size. One credit will usually take around ten hours of learning. Individual units make up full qualifications, either an Award, Certificate or Diploma, depending on the number of credits achieved. Units and qualifications are at a given level depending on the level of difficulty, from entry level to level 8.

The National Qualifications Framework (NQF) also groups qualifications together based on the level of difficulty from entry level to level 8. Ofqual provides an overview of the different qualifications and how they compare to general qualifications such as GCSEs and A levels, provided in Table 1.2.

Extension Activity

The register of regulated qualifications contains details of all the recognised awarding organisations and regulated qualifications in England, Wales and Northern Ireland. Go to http://register.ofqual.gov.uk and search for the vocational qualification you are currently teaching or are about to teach. What information does the register tell you? Which awarding organisation is the qualification with? Consider how this information will be essential to your planning, implementation and assessment.

Let's look at the main similarities and differences of each one and how this may impact on the way you teach and assess your vocational learners.

Apprenticeships

Apprenticeships provide both work-based experience and training to those over 16. Apprentices are employees who work alongside experienced staff to gain the skills they need to do the job. They also attend regular training, often one day away from their job, to develop underpinning knowledge and understanding.

Apprenticeships can take between one and four years to complete depending on the level of study. A range of qualifications make up a full 'apprenticeship framework' depending on the level and existing prior learning. These usually include a competence-based qualification (such as an NVQ), a knowledge-based qualification (such as a work-related technical certificate) and functional skills in Maths and English. Apprentices also develop their wider skills in relation to employee rights and responsibilities and personal learning and thinking skills (PLTS).

Key facts:

- Learners gain job-specific skills.

- Learners earn a salary and get paid holidays.

- Learners receive training and gain a range of qualifications that make up the apprenticeship framework.

Apprenticeships are available at three different levels: Intermediate (Level 2); Advanced (Level 3) and Higher (Level 4), in a wide range of subjects area, including:

- Agriculture, Horticulture and Animal Care;

- Arts, Media and Publishing;

- Business, Administration and Law;

- Construction, Planning and the Built Environment;

- Education and Training;

- Engineering and Manufacturing Technologies;

- Health, Public Services and Care;

- Information and Communication Technology;

- Leisure, Travel and Tourism;

- Retail and Commercial Enterprise.

Find out more: www.apprenticeships.org.uk

Traineeships

Introduced in August 2013, and seen as preparation for an apprenticeship programme, traineeships support young people (16–19-year-olds and young people with learning difficulties up to 25) to develop the skills they need to secure and succeed in employment.

Traineeships are aimed at young people who:

- are not currently in a job and have little work experience, but who are focused on work or the prospect of it;

- are qualified below Level 3; and

- providers and employers believe have a reasonable chance of being ready for employment or an apprenticeship within six months of engaging in a traineeship.

Completed within six months, traineeships provide learners with a substantial work placement (between six weeks and five months) with a guaranteed interview following at the end of the placement. This will be supported by work skills training, alongside English and Maths support, to develop learners' skills to progress quickly onto an apprenticeship or secure other employment.

Work-related qualifications

Work-related qualifications are designed to develop learners' knowledge, understanding and skills in a specific employment sector, for example, business and finance or health and social care. Qualifications are practical and include a range of units to give learners a broad understanding of the industries within a specific sector.

Popular work-related qualifications include BTECs and OCR Nationals. BTECs (originating from the founding organisation, the Business and Technology Education Council) are awarded by the Edexcel awarding organisation, part of the Pearson Education Group. BTECs are available as part of the QCF NQF and can be assessed through coursework or some now feature external assessment. More information on the assessment of vocational qualifications is explored in Chapters 7 and 8.

OCR Nationals are also industry-relevant qualifications offered at a range of levels and are often taken by learners in schools, colleges and training providers. Work-related qualifications offer progression across a large range of levels. To find out more, visit: www.edexcel.com/BTEC and www.ocr.org.uk/qualifications/by-type/ocr-nationals

National Vocational Qualifications (NVQs)

NVQs are flexible, competency-based qualifications based on the national occupation standards for a specific job role. They are usually completed in the workplace or settings that replicate the working environment. Learners are assessed on their ability to demonstrate their skills in carrying out job-specific tasks. A portfolio of evidence is collated to prove that learners are competent against the minimum standards required.

As a tutor or practitioner in FE and Skills, part of your role may well be as an assessor, making judgements on your learner's ability to meet the standards required for each unit in an NVQ qualification.

A huge range of careers are supported by NVQs including:

Advice and Guidance	Hairdressing and Barbering
Assessing and Assuring Quality	Health and Safety
Assessor and Verifier Awards	Housing
Brewing	Laundry Operations
Business and Administration	Logistics and Distributive Operations
Cleaning	Meat and Poultry Skills
Custodial Care	Providing Financial Advice
Customer Service	Road Passenger Transport

Driving Goods Vehicles	Security
Food Manufacturing	Telesales
Gambling Operations	Warehousing and Storage

Examples of NVQs include the City and Guilds Level 2 Award in Cleaning and Support Services Skills or the NCFE Level 2 NVQ Certificate In Team Leading.

Vocationally Related Qualifications (VRQs)

Unlike competency-based qualifications, Vocationally Related Qualifications (VRQs) are qualifications that relate to a specific occupational area, providing learners with the theoretical knowledge behind their chosen occupation. They can be taken by learners already working in the industry or hoping to change careers or enter employment in the sector.

Learners are often assessed through written assignments and projects, to evidence their developing levels of knowledge and understanding.

Examples of VRQs include the VTCT Level 3 VRQ in Women's Hairdressing or the IMI Level 2 VRQ in Motor Vehicle Studies.

Applied A levels and Applied GCSEs

GCSEs and A levels are subject to reform but are well known general qualifications, usually assessed through examination or a mix of exam and coursework. Applied versions of selected vocational GCSEs and A levels were developed to provide learners with a broad introduction to a specific vocational area, for example leisure studies or performing arts.

Technical Baccalaureate (TechBacc)

To be introduced from September 2014, the Technical Baccalaureate comprises three main elements:

- a high-quality Level 3 vocational qualification;

- a Level 3 core maths qualification, including AS level maths;

- an extended project – to develop and test students' skills in extended writing, communication, research, and self-discipline and self-motivation.

It is hoped that the Technical Baccalaureate will raise the status of vocational and technical education and qualifications at Level 3, providing learners with progression opportunities to a higher level apprenticeship, employment or university.

The range of different qualifications highlights the broad range of vocational areas covered. Lucas, Spencer and Claxton (2012: 36) suggest that it can be helpful to classify this diverse range of subjects into three broad categories:

Physical materials	Bricklaying, plumbing, hairdressing, professional make-up
People	Nursing, hospitality, retail, care, financial advice
Symbols	Journalism, software development, graphic design, accountancy

The Office for Standards in Education (Ofsted) divides the range of subjects into 15 sector subject areas (SSA), for the purposes of managing the inspections process. Table 1.1 highlights the prominence of vocational education in the FE and Skills sector.

Table 1.1   Subjects by sector area

Sector Subject Area (SSA)		
1. Health, public services and care	1.1	Medicine and dentistry
	1.2	Nursing and subjects and vocations allied to medicine
	1.3	Health and social care
	1.4	Public services
	1.5	Child development and well-being
2. Science and mathematics	2.1	Science
	2.2	Mathematics and statistics
3. Agriculture, horticulture and animal care	3.1	Agriculture
	3.2	Horticulture and forestry
	3.3	Animal care and veterinary science
	3.4	Environmental conservation
4. Engineering and manufacturing technologies	4.1	Engineering
	4.2	Manufacturing technologies
	4.3	Transportation operations and maintenance
5. Construction, planning and the built environment	5.1	Architecture
	5.2	Building and construction
	5.3	Urban, rural and regional planning
6. Information and communication technology	6.1	ICT practitioners
	6.2	ICT for users
7. Retail and commercial enterprise	7.1	Retailing and wholesaling
	7.2	Warehousing and distribution
	7.3	Service enterprises
	7.4	Hospitality and catering
8. Leisure, travel and tourism	8.1	Sport, leisure and recreation
	8.2	Travel and tourism
9. Arts, media and publishing	9.1	Performing arts
	9.2	Crafts, creative arts and design
	9.3	Media and communication
	9.4	Publishing and information services

(Continued)

Table 1.1   (Continued)

10. History, philosophy and theology	10.1	History
	10.2	Archaeology and archaeological sciences
	10.3	Philosophy
	10.4	Theology and religious studies
11. Social sciences	11.1	Geography
	11.2	Sociology and social policy
	11.3	Politics
	11.4	Economics
	11.5	Anthropology
12. Languages, literature and culture	12.1	Languages, literature and culture of the British Isles
	12.2	Other languages, literature and culture
	12.3	Linguistics
13. Education and training	13.1	Teaching and lecturing
	13.2	Direct learning support
14. Preparation for life and work	14.1	Foundations for learning and life
	14.1	Foundation English
	14.1	Foundation Mathematics
	14.1	Foundation English and Mathematics
	14.2	Preparation for work
	14.2	Foundation learning
15. Business, administration and law	15.1	Accounting and finance
	15.2	Administration
	15.3	Business management
	15.4	Marketing and sales
	15.5	Law and legal services

Extension Activity

Consider your own vocational subject area and explore the range of different accredited qualifications available.

- *Which Ofsted sector subject area (SSA) does your course fall into?*

- *What factors influence the choice of awarding organisation, qualification type and qualification size and what impact do these decisions have on your planning, delivery and implementation?*

- *Research the current debate around the type of vocational qualification you are teaching.*

- *Are there any proposed changes to the content or structure of the programme and what impacts will this have on you in meeting the needs of your learners and managing your workload?*

Table 1.2   Comparison of qualification levels (adapted from Ofqual, 2013)

Level	Qualifications examples	Framework for Higher Education examples
Entry	• Skills for Life at Entry level • Entry level awards, certificates and diplomas • Foundation Learning Tier pathways • Functional Skills at Entry level	
1	• GCSEs graded D–G • NVQs at Level 1 • Skills for Life • BTEC awards, certificates and diplomas at Level 1 • Functional Skills Level 1 • OCR Nationals • Foundation Learning Tier pathways	
2	• GCSEs graded A*–C • NVQs at Level 2 • Level 2 VQs • Skills for Life • BTEC awards, certificates and diplomas at Level 2 • Functional Skills Level 2	
3	• AS/A levels • Advanced Extension Awards • International Baccalaureate • NVQs at Level 3 • Level 2 VRQs • Cambridge International Awards • Advanced and Progression Diploma • Technical Baccalaureate • BTEC awards, certificates and diplomas at Level 3 • BTEC Nationals • OCR Nationals	
4	• NVQs at Level 4 • Certificates of higher education • Higher National Certificates (HNC) • BTEC Professional Diplomas, Certificates and Awards	• Certificates of higher education
5	• Higher National Diplomas (HND) • Other higher diplomas • BTEC Professional Diplomas, Certificates and Awards • NVQs at Level 5	• Diplomas of higher education and further education, Foundation degrees and Higher National Diplomas

(Continued)

Table 1.2 (Continued)

Level	Qualifications examples	Framework for Higher Education examples
6	• National Diploma in Professional Production Skills • BTEC Advanced Professional Diplomas, Certificates and Awards	• Bachelor degrees, graduate certificates and diplomas
7	• Postgraduate certificates and diplomas • BTEC advanced professional awards, certificates and diplomas • Fellowships and fellowship diplomas • Diploma in Translation • Advanced professional awards, certificates and diplomas	• Master's degrees, postgraduate certificates and diplomas
8	• Level 8 specialist awards • Award, certificate and diploma in strategic direction	• Doctorates

Adapted from: http://ofqual.gov.uk/qualifications-and-assessments/qualification-frameworks/levels-of-qualifications/

Case study

Meet Gwen, a 60-year-old social care worker.

I left school at 15 with virtually no qualifications. I enjoyed school but studying did not come easy to me. I left school and went to work as a clerk in a local factory before moving on to a retail job with Marks and Spencer. The training we received was very good, although there were no formal qualifications. After leaving work to bring up three children, I eventually returned to part-time work as a dinner-lady (I think they are called school welfare assistants now!). This was very enjoyable but there was only work in term-time and I was looking for more income.

Eventually I moved into a care assistant job at a local care home for the elderly. The work was hard but very rewarding. There was a change in the law and everyone needed to have a qualification in order to carry on working. My employer asked me to complete an NVQ2 in Health and Social Care. I remember feeling very anxious about having to complete forms and return to college. In the end, I didn't actually have to attend college at all. I was given an assessor who used to visit me regularly at the care home. She used to watch me carry out my duties and would complete observation records. We would also have 'professional discussions' where she would ask me questions about what I would do in different situations, what equipment I would use and what policies I would need to stick to.

I had to keep a portfolio of evidence and complete some small case studies. It was fascinating to realise how much knowledge and experience I had built up over the years and how much I was able to write! I began to enjoy learning and would look forward to the visit from my assessor. Well, I passed my Level 2. I decided to go straight on to my Level 3 qualification after encouragement from my assessor. I was so proud to receive a formal certification of my achievement. I showed it to my son who bought me a folder to store my certificates in. I was beginning to collect quite a few, after completing different short courses in first aid, moving and handling, safe handling of medicines and food hygiene. I realised that education was for me and I could be successful. The flexible format of the NVQ course allowed me to get credit for what I knew already and the skills I was using every day.

Activity

The format of the NVQ qualification provided flexibility for Gwen in her busy working day. What experiences and barriers to learning do your learners bring with them and how do you plan your teaching to meet these needs?

It is clear to see from the diverse range of qualifications, awarding organisations and frameworks that the vocational education landscape can be confusing to learners, tutors and parents. Each qualification specification sets out the content to be covered (what needs to be learnt) and what and how this will be assessed. The planning of learning to meet these specifications will be explored further in Chapter 5.

The range of vocational subjects to be taught again highlights how many practitioners and tutors in the further education and training sector have 'dual professionalism'; both as a teaching practitioner and as a subject expert. The Institute for Learning (IfL) highlights the importance of maintaining professional currency through continual professional development of both teacher and training skills and of subject-specific competences. Figure 1.1 below highlights various potential drivers for the professional development of vocational practitioners and tutors.

One way of maintaining your vocational currency, knowledge and skills is through engagement with the sector skills council, skills body or standards setting organisation. Most vocational subjects are represented by a skills organisation that leads the setting of national occupation standards to meet the needs of sector employers.

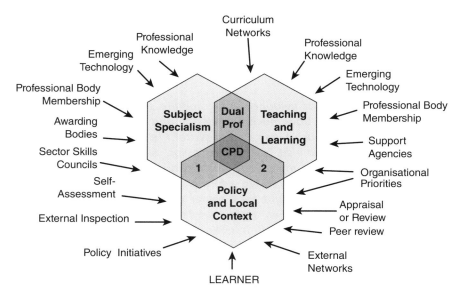

Figure 1.1   Dual professionalism and its impact on the model for continuing professional development:

1 relates to CPD arising out of subject specialism;

2 relates to CPD arising from teaching, and 1 and 2 both relate to the context in which you work. (Available from: http://www.ifl.ac.uk/__data/assets/pdf_file/0011/5501/J11734-IfL-CPD-Guidelines-08.09-web-v3.pdf)

Table 1.3   Sector skills councils, bodies and standards setting organisations

Sector skills councils, bodies and standards setting organisations	Sector coverage
Asset Skills http://www.assetskills.org	Property, housing, cleaning services, parking and facilities management
Cogent www.cogent-ssc.com	Bioscience, chemical, nuclear, oil and gas, petroleum and polymer industries
CITB www.citb.co.uk	Construction
Creative and Cultural Skills www.ccskills.org.uk	Craft, cultural heritage, design, literature, music, visual and performing arts.
e-skills UK www.e-skills.com	Information technology and telecommunications
Energy and Utility Skills www.euskills.co.uk	Electricity, gas, waste management and water industries
Financial Skills Partnership www.financialskillspartnership.org.uk	Financial services, finance and accounting sectors

Sector skills councils, bodies and standards setting organisations	Sector coverage
Improve www.improveltd.co.uk	Food and drink manufacturing and processing
Institute of the Motor Industry www.theimi.org.uk	The retail motor industry
Lantra www.lantra.co.uk	Environmental and land-based industries
People 1st www.people1st.co.uk	Hospitality, leisure, passenger transport, travel and tourism For more information read http://www.people1st.co.uk/hidden-section/Talent/2011/July-2011/People-1st-And-GoSkills-Are-Officially-One
Proskills UK www.proskills.co.uk	Process and manufacturing industry
SEMTA www.semta.org.uk	Science, engineering and manufacturing technologies (including composites)
Skills for Care and Development www.skillsforcareanddevelopment.org.uk	Early years, children and young people's services, and social work and social care for adults and children
Skills for Health www.skillsforhealth.org.uk	The health sector across the UK
Skills for Justice www.sfjuk.com	Community safety; courts, tribunals and prosecution; custodial care; fire and rescue; forensic science; law enforcement; legal services; offender management and support; policing; victim, survivor and witness support; youth justice and the children's workforce
Skills for Logistics www.skillsforlogistics.org	Freight logistics industry and wholesale
SkillsActive www.skillsactive.com	Active leisure, learning and well-being
Creative Skillset www.creativeskillset.org	Broadcast, fashion and textiles, film, video, interactive media, photo imaging, publishing and advertising
SummitSkills www.summitskills.org.uk	Building services, engineering
Skills CFA www.skillscfa.org	Business and administration
Habia www.habia.org	Hair, beauty, nails, spa therapy, barbering and African-Caribbean hairdressing

(Continued)

Table 1.3 (Continued)

Sector skills councils, bodies and standards setting organisations	Sector coverage
Sea Fish Industry Authority www.seafish.org	UK seafood industry
Institute of Customer Service www.instituteofcustomerservice. com	Customer service
Management Standard Centre www.management-standards.org	Management and leadership
Skills for Security www.skillsforsecurity.org.uk	Security business
Skills Third Sector www.skills-thirdsector.org.uk	Charities, social enterprises and the voluntary sector

Activity

Find the sector skills organisations relevant to the subjects that you teach or train. Explore the website and identify resources and sources of support that will help you bring your vocational subject to life.

Vocational pedagogy?

Given the distinction between general and vocational qualifications, does vocational education require a specific or distinct way of teaching? The word 'pedagogy' is often used to try to describe the art and science of teaching. Derived from the Greek 'to lead the child', the way we approach teaching and learning can be described as our pedagogy.

It could be viewed that many general subjects, such as traditional GCSEs and A levels are taught following a similar traditional, classroom-based style, leading to the end, or summative, exam. Tutors work hard to cover the necessary syllabus content and to prepare learners to answer examination questions in the best possible way to attract the best marks. Given the focus of vocational education on the real world of work and on applied, practical skills competence underpinned by subject-specific knowledge and understanding, do practitioners and tutors need to take a particular vocational approach to teaching, learning and assessment?

In their report 'It's all about work...', the Commission on Adult Vocational Teaching and Learning (CAVTL, 2013) identified eight distinctive features of adult vocational teaching and learning, or a 'vocational pedagogy':

1. that through the combination of sustained practice and the understanding of theory, occupational expertise is developed;

2. that work-related attributes are central to the development of occupational expertise;

3. that practical problem solving and critical reflection on experience, including learning from mistakes in real and simulated settings, are central to effective vocational teaching and learning;

4. that vocational teaching and learning is most effective when it is collaborative and contextualised, taking place within communities of practice which involve different types of 'teacher' and capitalise on the experience and knowledge of all learners;

5. that technology plays a key role because keeping on top of technological advances is an essential part of the occupational expertise required in any workplace;

6. that it requires a range of assessment and feedback methods that involve both 'teachers' and learners, and which reflect the specific assessment cultures of different occupations and sectors;

7. that it often benefits from operating across more than one setting, including a real or simulated workplace, as well as the classroom and workshop, to develop the capacity to learn and apply that learning in different settings, just as at work;

8. that occupational standards are dynamic, evolving to reflect advances in work practices, and that through collective learning, transformation in quality and efficiency is achieved.

Lucas, Spencer and Claxton (2012) identify that the main goal of vocational education is the development of 'working competence'; the ability and expertise to do skilful things to a set standard in a particular vocational area. This is different from the main objective of a general, more academic education where the main goal is to be able to write and talk about something. They identify six outcomes that are critical to developing and understanding working competence.

1. Routine expertise (being skilful).

2. Resourcefulness (stopping to think to deal with the non-routine).

3. Functional literacies (communication, and the functional skills of literacy, numeracy and ICT).

4. Craftsmanship (vocational sensibility; aspiration to do a good job; pride in a job well done).

5. Business-like attitudes (commercial or entrepreneurial sense – financial or social).

6. Wider skills for growth (for employability and lifelong learning).

Activity

Consider your own approach to teaching and training. Does your work prepare your learners to develop the six outcomes of working competence?

Think of an example of what you do in your practice for each of the six outcomes.

For example, as a tutor in hairdressing, Danny prepares his learners to develop routine expertise by demonstrating a range of popular cuts. After practising on training heads, learners develop their expertise in the college's working salon, with clients taking advantage of cheap prices. Danny is also on hand to support and develop learners' confidence in being resourceful and dealing with the non-routine, for example when a client has a specific need, a medical condition or a particular request.

It is really important for Danny's learners to develop their functional literacies. They have to be able to communicate with a range of customers in a professional way. They have to be able to operate office technology, handle money and perform calculations, for example when making up colouring solutions. Danny has high standards and has developed a good reputation after many years of owning his own salon. He works hard to stress the importance of craftsmanship to his own learners, to take time and pride in each client, to encourage repeat business and build up a loyal customer base.

Danny also recognises the need to develop learners' wider skills in business and commercial awareness, in order for them to be most employable and successful in a competitive market – skills such as up-selling (for example additional treatments and take-home products), working as part of an effective team, the ability to reflect and evaluate their own performance, and setting targets for future professional development.

A report following a study into effective vocational education (Faraday *et al.,* 2011) identified that there is little evidence of any fundamental differences between vocational teaching and learning and any other type of teaching and learning, except for 'context'. They define context as a range of different aspects, including:

- the nature of the vocational subject;

- the setting where teaching and learning takes place;

- objectives and desired outcomes for a session plus specifications of the qualification;

- the nature of the learners, their level and how they learn best including their learning styles.

Extension Activity

Consider each aspect of context and apply these to your own situation. How does the setting where you teach affect the way that you teach your vocational subject? Does this enhance learning or do you face restrictions and barriers to how you would ideally like to teach or train?

Consider the context of your learners. How do you find out about their prior knowledge and experiences? If they are adult learners, does their experience alter the way that you approach the planning of learning? Are there similarities or differences in the way they like to learn?

Vocational andragogy? A theory of adult vocational learning

Whilst discussing approaches to a vocational pedagogy, it is worth considering the much debated work of Malcolm Knowles and his theory of informal adult learning. Knowles popularised the debate around 'andragogy' and issues to consider when teaching adults as opposed to children and young people.

Knowles (1984) identified five key characteristics of adult learners:

1. Self-concept: As a person matures his self-concept moves from one of being a dependent personality toward one of being a self-directed human being.

2. Experience: As a person matures he accumulates a growing reservoir of experience that becomes an increasing resource for learning.

3. Readiness to learn: As a person matures his readiness to learn increasingly becomes oriented to the developmental tasks of his social roles.

4. Orientation to learning: As a person matures his time perspective changes from one of postponed application of knowledge to immediacy of application, and accordingly his learning orientation shifts from subject-centredness to problem-centredness.

5. Motivation to learn: As a person matures the motivation to learn is internal.

Activity

Consider each of the five key characteristics of adult learners. What potential implications does each characteristic have for the way that you plan, deliver and assess your vocational subject?

You might have identified some of the following considerations for your practice.

Learners are more motivated and autonomous and are able to be effective learners following independent study tasks, online or distance learning methods and choosing topics, units or modules of particular interest to themselves and their professional backgrounds. The scheme of work or curriculum plan should have flexibility to meet the individual needs and interests of adult learners who wish to learn at their own pace or in their own way.

Many adult vocational learners may have been working in or around the subject for many years, each with valuable experiences to share and ways of dealing with problems, overcoming barriers and tips and tricks for success. Lessons should provide time for valuing and sharing these experiences.

Many adult vocational learners may need to see very clearly how their studies link to their job and how it will help to solve problems and identify solutions to everyday issues they are facing in the workplace.

Whether we believe that vocational teaching and learning demands a specific pedagogy or andragogy to guide our approach, it seems clear that a focus on subject context, the real world of work and on developing our learners' practical, applied skills are appropriate considerations for teaching and training vocational learners.

Lucas, Spencer and Claxton (2012: 108) propose a useful five-step approach to considering the way we teach vocational education.

1. Be clear about the goal of vocational education.

2. Understand the nature of your subject.

3. Be clear about the breadth of desired outcomes.

4. Understand the range of learning methods that may, taken together, provide the best blend.

5. Bear in mind any contextual factors: the nature of learners; the expertise of the 'teacher'; and the setting for learning.

Reflection point

Reflect on your own view about the nature of vocational education and whether you feel a specific pedagogy is appropriate. What do you consider to be the most important factors when preparing to teach and train vocational learners?

The debate about the role, format and approach to teaching vocational education will continue and new initiatives, programmes and qualifications will continue to be developed. We explore this constantly changing landscape in the next chapter and advise all vocational practitioners and tutors to maintain clear sight of the critical role of vocational education and training in meeting the needs of learners and in developing the knowledge, understanding and skills required for a modern and competitive economy.

Summary

In this chapter we have looked at a number of key themes.

- *The complex nature of vocation education and training.*

- *The similarities and differences between general 'academic' and vocational qualifications.*

- *The range of vocational qualifications and contacts across the further education and training sector.*

- *Ideas for developing a vocational pedagogy or andragogy for effective teaching and training of vocational adults and young people.*

Theory focus

Further reading

CAVTL (Commission on Adult Vocational Teaching and Learning) (2013) *It's about work... Excellent Adult Vocational Teaching and Learning*. London: Learning and Skills Improvement Service.

Faraday, S, Overton, C and Cooper, S (2011) *Effective Teaching and Learning in Vocational Education*. London: LSN.

Gravells, A (2012) *Achieving your TAQA Assessor and Internal Quality Assurer Award*. Exeter: Learning Matters.

Lucas, B, Spencer, E and Claxton, G (2012) *How to Teach Vocational Education: A Theory of Vocational Pedagogy*. London: City and Guilds Centre for Skills Development.

Tummons, J (2007) *Becoming a Professional Tutor in the Lifelong Learning Sector*. Exeter: Learning Matters.

Websites

Centre for Real-World Learning: www.winchester.ac.uk/aboutus/lifelonglearning/ CentreforRealWorldLearning

Centre for Skills Development: www.skillsdevelopment.org

City and Guilds: www.cityandguilds.com

Department for Education: www.education.gov.uk

Edexcel: www.edexcel.com

Institute for Learning: www.ifl.ac.uk

Office of Qualifications and Examinations Regulation: http://ofqual.gov.uk

National Occupational Standards: http://nos.ukces.org.uk

Register of Regulated Qualifications: http://register.ofqual.gov.uk/

References

CAVTL (Commission on Adult Vocational Teaching and Learning) (2013) *It's about work... Excellent Adult Vocational Teaching and Learning*. London: Learning and Skills Improvement Service.

Faraday, S, Overton, C and Cooper, S (2011) *Effective Teaching and Learning in Vocational Education*. London: LSN.

Knowles, M and associates (1984) *Andragogy in Action. Applying Modern Principles of Adult Education*. San Francisco: Jossey Bass.

Lucas, B, Spencer, E and Claxton, G (2012) *How to Teach Vocational Education: A Theory of Vocational Pedagogy*. London: City and Guilds Centre for Skills Development.

Ofqual (2013) *Qualification Levels – Comparison of Qualification Levels Between the NQF and QCF Frameworks*. London: Ofqual. Available from: http://ofqual.gov.uk/qualifications-and-assessments/ qualification-frameworks/levels-of-qualifications (accessed 24 August 2013).

Richardson, W and Wiborg, S (2010) *English Technical and Vocational Education in Historical and Comparative Perspective. Considerations for University Technical Colleges*. London: Baker-Dearing Foundation.

Tummons, J (2007) *Becoming a Professional Tutor in the Lifelong Learning Sector*. Exeter: Learning Matters.

2 THE CHANGING LANDSCAPE

In this chapter you will learn about:

- changing policy and the impact on practice, including qualifications, tutor training and the role of work experience;
- changing costs and the opportunities provided through learning grants and the expansion of HE within FE;
- changing contexts, including the expansion of UTCs and studio schools;
- how to maintain currency with changes to the sector through engagement with education and training support organisations.

Professional Standards

Standard 10: Reflect on, develop and maintain own skills and practice in learning and development – KU5 How to find out about and stay abreast of trends and developments relevant to own skills, knowledge and practice including those relating to technological developments

Standard 13: Evaluate and improve learning and development provision – KU17 The impact of the wider learning environment on the learner experience

Introduction

The education system in the UK is a complex and dynamic system that seems ever changing. The rate and pace of change can be particularly felt in the area of vocational education and training. This chapter explores some of the recent drivers for change and how government policy has a significant impact on the daily working lives of vocational tutors and practitioners in schools, colleges and across the FE and Skills sector.

In a bid to improve the quality of FE and Skills training, successive UK governments have commissioned a variety of reviews and reports exploring how to make vocational education more efficient and more effective. These reports often lead to a series of recommendations that affect the roles of many VET practitioners across diverse contexts and settings. The FE and skills sector comprises more than 220 further education (FE) colleges, 900 independent training providers and around 2,500 training organisations. Vocational education and training is also carried out in a very diverse range of other organisations, including:

- secondary schools, academies and free-schools;
- universities;
- university technical colleges;
- sixth-form colleges;
- land-based colleges;
- specialist colleges;
- emergency and public services;
- armed forces;
- work-based learning providers;
- voluntary sector;
- adult and community learning providers;
- prison and offender learning.

Changing policy

In 2010 the UK government published two strategy documents, *Skills for Sustainable Growth* and *Investing in Skills for Sustainable Growth*, which identified a number of key reforms of further education for adults aged 19 and over. Following a public consultation and publication of the Wolf Review of Vocational Education, the strategy document *New Challenges, New Chances* outlined the government's plans to reform the FE and Skills sector. These reforms are part of the many changes that you will be dealing with as a practitioner and tutor in the sector.

By keeping up to date with the changes, you can ensure that your planning of teaching, learning and assessment continues to meet the demands of the sector, your employer and most importantly, the needs of your learners.

The Wolf Review of Vocational Education

As explored in Chapter 1, the review of vocational education in England by Professor Alison Wolf in 2011, identified a number of key recommendations, many of which have had a significant impact on qualifications, funding and study programmes for vocational learners.

Key recommendations in the report included:

- incentivising young people to take the most valuable vocational qualifications pre-16, while removing incentives to take large numbers of vocational qualifications to the detriment of core academic study;

- introducing principles to guide study programmes for young people on vocational routes post-16 to ensure they are gaining skills which will lead to progression into a variety of jobs or further learning, in particular, to ensure that those who have not secured a good pass in English and Mathematics GCSE continue to study those subjects;

- evaluating the delivery structure and content of apprenticeships to ensure they deliver the right skills for the workplace;

- making sure the regulatory framework moves quickly away from accrediting individual qualifications to regulating awarding organisations;

- removing the requirement that all qualifications offered to 14- to 19-year-olds fit within the Qualifications and Credit Framework, which has had a detrimental effect on their appropriateness and has left gaps in the market;

- enabling FE lecturers and professionals to teach in schools, ensuring young people are being taught by those best suited.

Reflection point

If you have been teaching and training in vocational education for some time, you may have felt directly the impact of some of these recommendations on your current practice. Consider what these changes have meant for you. Do you agree with the recommendations and the resulting changes to both policy and practice?

In April 2012, the government introduced regulations to allow those holding Qualified Teacher Learning and Skills (QTLS) status to teach vocational courses in schools. QTLS is currently awarding by the Institute for Learning (IfL) through a process of professional formation, where qualified lecturers and trainers demonstrate how they meet the professional standards expected in the sector.

The vast number of accredited vocational qualifications has been criticised as many were thought not to provide vocational learners with the challenge and rigour required to develop knowledge, skills and understanding appropriately to lead to progression. As of September 2013, all post-16 schools, colleges and work-based learning providers are now responsible for planning the delivery of study programmes, based on learners' prior attainment and their career and educational aspirations. Vocational study programmes must include a 'substantial' qualification from an approved awarding organisation.

Each study programme should:

- provide progression to a level higher than that of learners' prior attainment;

- include qualifications that are of sufficient size and rigour to stretch learners and are clearly linked to suitable progression opportunities in training, employment or higher levels of education;

- require learners to work towards GCSE A*–C grade in Maths and English, or other qualifications such as Functional Skills that will act as a stepping stone for achievement;

- allow for meaningful work experience related to the vocational area of the study programme, which develops employability skills and/or creates potential employment options;

- include other activities unrelated to qualifications that develop the skills, attitudes and confidence that support progression.

Activity

Consider your own professional context. Are you teaching or training learners on a specific study programme? Which aspects of the programme are you responsible for? Do you feel the programme is sufficiently challenging and preparing your learners to progress to employment or higher level study? Are you expected to develop your own learners' English and mathematics skills?

The value of vocational work experience

A significant part of learners' study programmes is now a period of 'meaningful' work experience. Rather than simply carrying out basic and menial tasks in a standard two-week block of work placement, the experience should be valuable and give learners an excellent introduction to the world of work in a specific sector.

The Department for Education (2013) has provided guidelines on how to ensure learners receive a good quality work experience placement, either experiential (short periods of work experience sometimes exploring different vocations through study visits, engagement with employers and projects) or vocational (experience focused on a specific vocational area which contributes directly to learners' study programmes).

Meaningful work experience:

- is purposeful, substantial, offers challenge and is relevant to the young persons' study programme and/or career aspirations;

- is managed well under the direction of a supervisor in order to ensure that the learner obtains a genuine learning experience suited to their needs;

- ensures that time is well spent: the employer has prepared a structured plan for the duration of the work placement that provides tangible outcomes for the learner and employer;

- provides up-front clarity about the roles, responsibilities and the expectations of the learner and employer;

- is reviewed at the end: the employer provides some form of reference or feedback based on the young person's performance during their time on the work placement.

UXBRIDGE COLLEGE
LEARNING CENTRE

Activity

Many vocational qualifications include a specific unit on developing employ-ability skills through work experience. Learners are often required to plan, participate and evaluate a period of sector-specific work experience.

Explore the qualifications specification for your own subject. Is there a unit of study that would help to support and structure a period of work experience?

What do you consider the difficulties to be in ensuring every learner is able to complete a period of meaningful work experience on their study programme?

Changes to the funding of study programmes have led to an increased focus on enter-prise education in schools and colleges. Learners on vocational programmes particularly should have the opportunity to participate in a wide range of enterprise activities, such as workplace visits, workshops and projects. Engagement with employers and enterprise is discussed further in Chapter 4.

Many of the different vocational qualifications explored in Chapter 1 can contribute to a 16–19 study programme, including traineeships, apprenticeships and work-related quali-fications. Traditionally, many work-related qualifications, such as BTECs, were assessed internally through coursework assignments. A recommendation in the Wolf Review to improve the rigour of many vocational qualifications includes the introduction of an ele-ment of external assessment, such as an exam. Vocational assessment is explored further in Chapter 7.

The Richard Review of Apprenticeships

The form of vocational education and training known as an 'apprenticeship' has been well known for many years. Often traditionally associated with the trade professions, such as bricklaying, carpentry and joinery, plumbing and electrical work, undertaking an appren-ticeship was historically seen as a sound practical progression option for many school leavers.

Under successive governments the form and content of apprenticeships has changed dra-matically. More recently, the number of apprenticeships has expanded. There are over 100,000 employers offering nearly 250 apprenticeship frameworks, across 1,200 job roles. Apprenticeships are now available at different levels and cover a diverse range of occupa-tions such as dental nursing, graphic design, horticulture, electric vehicle engineering and creative and digital media.

In November 2012, the government commissioned entrepreneur Doug Richard to com-plete a review of apprenticeships. His review made a number of recommendations, which are being used to re-shape the format and increase the status of apprenticeship pro-grammes in England. His recommendations include:

- Redefining apprenticeships – so that they target only those who are new to a job or role that requires sustained and substantial training. Training for those already in a job is classed as vocational training.

- Focusing on the outcome of an apprenticeship – what the apprentice can do when they complete their training – and freeing up the process by which they get there. Trusted, independent assessment is seen as key.

- Recognised industry standards should form the basis of every apprenticeship.

- All apprentices should reach a good level in English and maths before they can complete their apprenticeship.

- Government funding must create the right incentives for apprenticeship training. The purchasing power for investing in apprenticeship training should lie with the employer.

- Greater diversity and innovation in training – with employers and government safeguarding quality.

Reflection point

Are you involved in teaching and training learners on apprenticeship programmes? What changes have you noticed and how do they impact on your working practice? Do you feel apprenticeships are high quality and attract the status of courses following more 'academic' routes, progressing to university-based education programmes?

Professionalism in further education

The status and professional nature of practitioners and tutors in the FE and Skills sector has long been a topic of great debate. For many years, FE lecturers were employed on very different terms and conditions to their schoolteacher counterparts. The nature of being 'qualified' to teach in the sector has also undergone significant change.

Following the introduction of Qualified Teacher Learning and Skills (QTLS) status, many vocational education professionals enjoyed the recognition of a formal qualified status, awarded by the Institute for Learning (IfL) following a process of 'professional formation'.

In October 2012, the final report of the independent review panel was published. 'Professionalism in Further Education', chaired by Lord Lingfield, set out a number of recommendations to reform and simplify the arrangements for FE initial teacher education. These changes are on-going, including the introduction of new teacher training qualifications, a review of FE professional standards and the impact of the Education and Training Foundation. Regulations from 2007 which required FE teachers and trainers to have a recognised teaching qualification, were revoked in September 2013, although most providers currently still insist tutors complete a qualification.

The new qualifications for FE and Skills practitioners replace those previously known as PTTLS, CTLLS and DTLLS and include three generic initial teacher training (ITT) qualifications: a Level 3 Award in Education and Training, a Level 4 Certificate in Education and Training, and a Level 5 Diploma in Education and Training. Specialist qualifications are also available at Level 5 for those teaching English (Literacy), ESOL, mathematics and disabled learners.

Educators have the opportunity to undertake ITT qualifications through an awarding organisation route (for example with City and Guilds, Edexcel (Pearson) or Ascentis) or for those studying at the higher levels, through a university provider.

Reflection point

As a vocational specialist, you are likely to be very experienced and highly qualified in your specialist subject. Becoming an educator in your subject leads to a new role as a dual professional as discussed in Chapter 1.

Within your education role, are you qualified, part way through completing a qualification or unqualified? Do you feel that you should be required to complete a qualification in education and training in order to teach your vocational subject?

Changing costs

As the costs of higher education continue to rise, many learners are looking for more cost-effective study options, including 'HE in FE'. Many further education providers now offer substantial study programmes for higher education courses in vocational subjects, including higher national certificates and diplomas (HNC/Ds) and foundation degrees. The opportunity to study more locally, in smaller groups with accessible lecturers and at a cheaper rate than universities means that HE in FE is a significant area for growth.

'Advanced Learning Loans' are now available to help learners aged 24 or above pay the fees charged by colleges and training providers for higher level courses at Level 3 and Level 4, or for Advanced and Higher Apprenticeships.

Similar to the student loans scheme for higher education, learners do not have to repay the loan until they are earning over £21,000 a year. A bursary fund is also often available to assist learners with childcare or residential costs.

Extension Activity

Carry out some research into HE in FE opportunities in your local area. Compare the costs associated with study in an FE environment compared to those offered by universities.

Would you be prepared to teach your vocational subject at Levels 4 and 5? What professional development might you need to undertake in order to deliver excellent teaching, learning and assessment on higher education programmes?

Changing contexts

As well as changes to policy and funding, where learners can study vocational education and training programmes has also changed. The FE and Skills sector is already very diverse, with colleagues working in a great variety of public, private, voluntary and charitable organisations. More options than ever before are now available to the vocational learner, with many secondary schools offering vocational options from Year 9 (aged 13) onwards.

University Technical Colleges (www.utcolleges.org)

Over 30 University Technical Colleges (UTCs) were founded in England in 2011/12, providing a mix of practical and academic studies for learners aged 14–19. Approval for 45 UTCs is now in place. Each UTC is sponsored by a university and specialises in two distinct areas, for example, engineering, product design, health sciences, construction, and land and environmental services.

By combining support from local employers and academic rigour from the university partner, qualifications provided by UTCs may be highly regarded and offer clear progression routes into higher education or further learning in work.

Studio schools (www.studioschoolstrust.org)

Studio schools, developed by the Studio Schools Trust, in partnership with the Department for Education, and local and national education providers and employers, are small schools of around 300 learners. Over 40 studio schools in England offer mainstream qualifications (including GCSEs, A levels, and vocational and professional qualifications) linked to the world of work, and focused on developing the employability and life skills required by employers.

Like UTCs, many also have a specialism linked to their local employer base, including creative and digital technologies, Science Technology Engineering and Maths (STEM), health and social care and sport. Learners at a studio school develop employability and life skills through the CREATE skills framework:

Communication – to be able to convey information and ideas so they are received and understood by others.

Relating to people – to be able to successfully interact with others in a range of roles and situations.

Enterprise – to develop, implement and learn from ideas.

Applied skills – to be able to effectively apply skills to a variety of situations and contexts.

Thinking skills – to be able to process ideas to make reasoned judgements and solve problems.

Emotional intelligence – to understand and manage the emotions of self and others.

Enterprise academies (www.pjea.org.uk)

Founded in 2009 by Peter Jones CBE, entrepreneur and star of the BBC enterprise programme *Dragons' Den*, over 38 education providers are offering vocational courses in enterprise and employability through enterprise academies. Each academy works closely with local and national businesses in order to develop learners' skills to progress and succeed in the world of business.

Both younger learners and adults can choose from a range of different enterprise and entrepreneurship courses, including BTECs, short courses and apprenticeships at different levels. Courses are supplemented by a range of work-related activities and experiences, including:

- master classes;
- work experience;
- entrepreneurial learning;
- business challenges;
- workshops;
- company visits;
- scholarships.

Blended and distance learning

As many institutions look to achieve efficiencies on their traditional curriculum models in the light of challenging funding models, more and more vocational education providers are exploring the role of distance and blended learning opportunities. Blended learning is a combination of traditional face-to-face teaching with online learning, often offered through a virtual learning environment (VLE) such as Moodle or Blackboard.

Blended and online learning options offer a number of advantages as well as challenges for vocational practitioners and their institutions. The Joint Information Systems Committee (JISC, 2010) highlights how effective e-learning used well has a number of benefits for learners. It:

- engages learners in the learning process;
- encourages independent learning skills;
- develops learners' skills and knowledge;
- motivates further learning.

Done well, blended learning opportunities may well enhance the quality and accessibility of many vocational programmes, allowing learners to work from home, to access rich and engaging multimedia and learn in a multi-model way. If blended and online learning is now good quality, it may have significant consequences for levels of learner motivation and engagement, which are topics explored further in Chapter 3.

As a vocational tutor, you will also need to be aware of your own skills and competencies with regard to e-learning, the use of VLEs and multimedia resources. It is fast becoming a minimum expectation of all vocational practitioners to have a good working knowledge of learning technologies.

Case study

Delivery efficiencies of up to 15 per cent have been made on all full-time Level 2 and 3 courses at Worcester College of Technology. They developed a Personally Accountable Learning (PAL) model to provide a range of online materials and support through the college's Moodle VLE. PAL packs were developed through a partnership between tutors, learning technologists and quality assurance staff to offer learners high quality independent learning activities, including quizzes, discussion forums, multimedia resources and assessments.

For more information, visit: http://diglit.wortech.ac.uk

Extension Activity

Take a skills assessment in ICT to identify your own areas of strength and areas for development with the use of technology: http://keyskillstrainer.excellence-gateway.org.uk/login.html

On completion, consider setting targets for how you can improve your level of ICT competence in order to better support your vocational learners in a digital knowledge age.

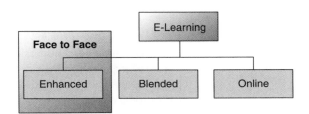

Figure 2.1   A continuum of e-learning based on Garrison and Kanuka (2004)

Maintaining currency

We have explored how the vocational education and training landscape has, and continues, to change and evolve at a rapid pace. It is challenging for even the most experienced education practitioner to maintain a working knowledge of all these changes and to prepare for the impact that these changes and opportunities bring.

It is important to seek support from a large number of organisations across the FE and Skills landscape and to maintain your awareness of the latest changes to policy, qualifications, careers and funding, to ensure you can best advise and prepare your learners.

Table 2.1   Resources for maintaining currency in the FE landscape

Times Education Supplement (TES) www.tes.co.uk	Published each Friday, the *TES* includes a specific section related to further education and reports on major news stories from across the sector.
FE Week www.feweek.co.uk	Aimed at middle and senior management working in colleges and private training providers, *FE Week* is published weekly in term-time, providing news, comment and technical information on the sector.
Edexcel Policy Watch www.edexcel.com	Sign up to receive updates on policy and funding from one of the largest awarding organisations.
Broadsheet from City and Guilds www.cityandguilds.com	Reporting on the latest news, qualifications and services from the City and Guilds Group, *Broadsheet* magazine provides features, comment and analysis for the vocational education sector.
FE News www.fenews.co.uk	*FE News* is a further education, skills and work-based learning online news magazine
Journal of Vocational Education and Training www.tandfonline.com	An academic journal published four times per year featuring the latest research in the area of vocational education and training from across the world.
The Edge Foundation www.twitter.com/ukedge	Follow the Edge Foundation on Twitter and keep up to date on the sector through their Twitter micro-blogging service.
Innovation in Vocational Education and Training www.linkedin.com	An online members' discussion area of the professional networking site LinkedIn. Members from across the world discuss issues relating to vocational education and training.

Make good use of the range of support organisations across the FE and Skills sector, as well as departments and professional development opportunities within your own institution.

Table 2.2   Summary of FE and skills organisations

Education and Training Foundation (ETF) www.et-foundation.co.uk	The Education and Training Foundation is responsible for setting and maintaining the professional standards and code of practice for those working in the Further Education and Skill sector, along with developing qualifications for initial teacher training.
Education Business Partnerships (EBPs)	The UK has a network of over 100 privately funded education business partnerships designed to support opportunities for businesses and young people to work together. The services of EBPs are often used by schools and colleges to arrange work experience placements, carry out risk assessments of placement providers and to deliver enterprise education.
Local Enterprise Partnerships (LEPs) www.lepnetwork.org.uk	LEPs are partnerships between local authorities and businesses. There are 39 LEPs across England, many of which are leading an 'enterprise zone'. Replacing regional development agencies, LEPs make decisions on the priorities for investment in roads, buildings and facilities in their local area. The 2010 White Paper 'Local Growth' set out the role of LEPs, including their role to work with local education providers to support local economic development.
Association of Employment and Learning Providers (AELP) www.aelp.org.uk	AELP is a trade association for vocational learning and employment providers in Britain. Most of its members are independent, private, not-for-profit and voluntary sector training and employment services organisations. The majority of apprenticeships in England are delivered by AELP members.
Federation for Industry Sector Skills and Standards www.fisss.org	The Federation co-ordinates the quality assurance and certification of apprenticeships on behalf of the Skills Funding Agency, the National Apprenticeship Service and employers. It works with the sector skills councils to support, develop and implement a code of practice.

(Continued)

Table 2.2   (Continued)

Sector skills councils, bodies and standards setting organisations	There are a range of independent, employer-led sector skills councils (SCCs) and sector skills bodies that define and develop skills and standards for their industry. For more information, see Table 1.3 in Chapter 1.
National Apprenticeship Service (NAS) www.apprenticeships.org.uk	The NAS supports, funds and co-ordinates the delivery of apprenticeships throughout England. It has a responsibility to increase the number of apprenticeship opportunities and support both employers and learners through advertising apprenticeship vacancies. NAS also manages 'World Skills UK', a range of vocational skills competitions and activities.
The UK Commission for Employment and Skills www.ukces.org.uk	UKCES is a publicly funded, industry-led organisation providing strategic leadership on skills and employment issues in the UK. The commission carries out research and publishes a range of reports on the UK employment and skills sector and the impact on vocational education and training sector.
Institute for Learning (IfL) www.ifl.ac.uk	The IfL is the independent professional body for practitioners, tutors and student teachers in the Further Education (FE) and Skills sector. The IfL aims to support its members through continuing professional development (CPD) activities and representing the sector through engagement with policy.
Chartered Institute of Educational Assessors www.ciea.co.uk	The CIEA is a professional membership organisation providing advice, information and training to those involved with educational assessment, including tutors, assessors, examiners and verifiers.
Office for Qualifications and Examination Regulation (Ofqual) www.ofqual.gov.uk	Independent of government, Ofqual is the regulator of qualifications, examinations and assessments in England and vocational qualifications in Northern Ireland. Their role is to maintain standards and confidence in qualifications, through accreditation and monitoring of awarding organisations.

Office for Standards in Education, Children's Services and Skills (Ofsted) www.ofsted.gov.uk	Ofsted inspects and regulates services that care for children and young people, and those providing education and skills for learners of all ages. Publicly funded education organisations will be subject to an Ofsted inspection, where judgements are made against a Common Inspection Framework (CIF). Public reports on the quality of education and training providers are published on the Ofsted website.
Federation of Awarding Bodies (FAB) www.fab.org.uk	FAB is a trade association for vocational awarding bodies in the UK. It represents over 120 awarding bodies, providing information, advice and guidance to members and contributing to consultations by the government and the regulator.
Department for Business, Skills and Innovation (BIS) http://bis.gov.uk	BIS is the UK government department for economic growth. Part of the department's role is to promote trade and innovation through investment in skills and education.
Skills Funding Agency (SFA) http://skillsfundingagency.bis.gov.uk	A partner organisation to the Department for Business, Innovation and Skills (BIS), the SFA funds adult further education (FE) and skills training in England.
Education Funding Agency (EFA) www.education.gov.uk/aboutdfe/executiveagencies/efa	The EFA is an executive agency for the Department of Education. The agency administers education funding for learners between the ages of 3 and 19, or up to 25 for those with special educational needs and disabilities.
Business in the Community (BITC) www.bitc.org.uk	A business-led charity, BITC works with businesses to build links with schools to provide support and resources for enterprise and employability. BITC co-ordinate the government-endorsed programme 'Business First'.
Learning Records Service (LRS) www.learningrecordsservice.org.uk	The LRS co-ordinates information and data on individual learning providers, learners' unique learner number (ULN) and the personal learning record (PLR). The service is designed to make it easier for both learning providers and learners themselves to track and record what learning has taken place and when. Learners can access their own PLR through the National Careers Service website.

(Continued)

Table 2.2   (Continued)

Centre for Skills Development (CSD) www.skillsdevelopment.org	Part of the City and Guilds group, the Centre for Skills Development is a not-for-profit, research and development organisation for vocational education and training. The centre works with researchers and practitioners to influence and improve the policy and practice of vocational education and training. The centre's website offers practitioners a range of publications, reports and toolkits for working with vocational learners.
National Careers Service (NCS) https://nationalcareersservice.direct.gov.uk	Supported by qualified careers advisers, the NCS provides information, advice and guidance to help adults and young people make decisions on learning, training and work opportunities. The website has a range of career tools and allows learners to open a lifelong learning account and check their personal learning record.
National Institute of Adult Continuing Education (NIACE) www.niace.org.uk	Through a range of events, research, publications and support services, NIACE aims to encourage all adults to engage in learning of all kinds. NIACE also runs the Adult Learners' Week campaign.
Land Based College Aspiring To Excellence (Landex) www.landex.org.uk	Membership organisation representing colleges offering land-based occupations.
Holex www.excellencegateway.org.uk	HOLEX is the sector membership body for local authority adult and community learning (ACL) services.
European Prison Education Association www.epea.org	The EPEA is an organisation made up of prison tutors and other professionals whose interests lie in promoting and developing education in prisons throughout Europe.
Third Sector National Learning Alliance (TSNLA) www.tsnla.org.uk	TSNLA is a national alliance of voluntary, community organisations and social enterprises involved in learning and skills.
The Further Education Reputation Strategy Group (FERSG) www.feworks.org	FERSG is a sector-led group that aims to enhance the national reputation of further education (FE). Its programme of activities involve raising issues affecting the sector's reputation with the government, cross-sector meetings and research projects.
Sixth Form Colleges' Association (SFCA) www.sixthformcolleges.org	SFCA represents, supports and promotes the interests of the sixth-form college sector.

Association of Colleges (AoC) www.aoc.co.uk	Established in 1996, the AoC represents and promotes the interests of colleges and provides members with professional support services.
National Training Federation Wales (NTfW) www.ntfw.org	NTfW is a Wales-wide membership organisation for those involved in the delivery of learning in the workplace. Members range from small specialist training providers to national and international organisations, as well as local authorities, further education institutions and charities.

Summary

In this chapter we have looked at a number of key themes:

- *changing policy and the impact on practice, including qualifications, teacher training and the role of work experience;*

- *changing costs and the opportunities provided through learning grants and the expansion of HE within FE;*

- *changing contexts, including the expansion of UTCs and studio schools;*

- *how to maintain currency with changes to the sector through engagement with education and training support organisations.*

Theory focus

Further reading

BIS (2012) *Professionalism in Further Education: Final Report of the Independent Review Panel.* London: Department for Business, Innovation and Skills.

DFE/BIS (2011) *New Challenges, New Chances: Further Education and Skills System Reform Plan: Building a World Class Skills System.* London: Department for Business, Innovation and Skills.

DFE/BIS (2013) *Rigour and Responsiveness in Skills.* London: Department for Business, Innovation and Skills. London: Department for Business, Innovation and Skills.

DFE/BIS (2013) *Traineeships – Supporting young people to develop the skills for Apprenticeships and other sustained jobs: a discussion paper.* London: Department for Business, Innovation and Skills.

Duckworth, V and Tummons, J (2010) *Contemporary Issues in the Lifelong Learning Sector.* Maindenhead: Open University Press.

Richard, D (2012) *The Richard Review of Apprenticeships.* London: School for Startups.

Wolf, A (2011) *Review of Vocational Education – The Wolf Report.* London: The Stationery Office.

Websites

Edexcel: www.edexcel.com

City and Guilds: www.cityandguilds.com

Department for Education: www.education.gov.uk

Institute for Learning: www.ifl.ac.uk

Edge Foundation: www.edge.co.uk

FE Week: www.feweek.co.uk

FE News: www.fenews.co.uk

References

DFE (2013) *Work Experience and Non-qualification Activity*. Available from: www.education.gov.uk/600223495/post-16-work-exp-enteprise-educ

Garrison, D R and Kanuka, H (2004) 'Blended Learning: Uncovering its Transformative Potential in Higher Education', *The Internet and Higher Education*, 7(2): 95–105.

Richard, D (2012) *The Richard Review of Apprenticeships*. London: School for Start ups.

In this chapter you will learn about:

- the behaviourist, cognitivist and humanistic approaches to learning;
- theories of motivation and considerations for your practice;
- creating safe and secure learning environments through equality and diversity;
- differences between a fixed and a growth mindset;
- ways to differentiate your approach to learning;
- the importance of feedback, choice and optimal challenge for motivation.

Professional Standards

Standard 2: Identify individuals' learning and development needs – KU2 Why it is important to identify a learner's objectives and motivation to learn when analysing their learning needs

Standard 6: Manage learning and development in groups – KU11 The types of motivational strategies that would support group and individual learning and how to select these according to identified needs

Standard 7: Facilitate individual learning and development – KU1 The principles, uses and value of learning and development on an individual basis

Standard 8: Engage and support learners in the learning and development process – KU4 Aspects of equality and diversity that need to be addressed when supporting learners

Introduction

In Chapters 1 and 2 we have explored different perspectives and definitions of what vocational education and training is, and the qualifications, organisations, policies and contexts that shape the work of vocational tutors across the country.

In this chapter, we focus on vocational learners and the need to develop and enhance your approaches to vocational teaching, learning and assessment. Your aim as a vocational practitioner is to CHIME with all your learners:

- **C**ommunicate;

- **H**elp;

- **I**nspire;

- **M**otivate;

- **E**ngage.

The need to 'CHIME'

The UK Commission for Employment and Skills (UKCES) identifies that the number of young people not in education, employment or training (so called NEETs) now stands at around 1.5 million; 1 in 5 of all young people. They predict that by 2022 this will result in £28 billion in costs to the exchequer in lost output to the economy, on top of the human and social costs that result from not being engaged in meaningful employment or study (www.ukces.org.uk/ourwork/outcome-two#).

Too many young people leave school without formal qualifications. For many of those disaffected with a traditional school education, vocational skills training provides a new and exciting way to learn in a more accessible environment. With a clear purpose and focus on developing real world skills for jobs, vocational education and training can provide the framework for social, personal and academic development.

Colleges, prisons, work-based learning providers and charities all need to offer supportive, nurturing and challenging learning experiences. For many young people, opportunities to engage with a vocational study programme have been made easier, with colleges now able to recruit learners aged 14 directly.

Of course adult vocational learners also need engaging and motivating practitioners and tutors. Many are returning to education after many years and some will have had very negative prior learning experiences. They may well arrive in your classroom, salon or workshop after 30 years of no formal qualifications and a history of non-achievement or no formal success.

Others will have a long history of success but are looking to further their careers or move sectors. They may well arrive in your IT room, studio or sports hall after a long day at work. They will need inspiring and helpful tutors to challenge and engage them to give up their precious personal time to complete their part-time vocational studies.

A question of motivation

Learner motivation refers to the *willingness, need, desire and compulsion to participate in, and be successful in, the learning process* (Bomia et al., 1997: 294). When considering approaches to engage and motivate our learners, it is worth considering different approaches, or orientations to learning. Educational psychologists have proposed a number of different explanations, or theories, for why and how we learn. The impact of these theories can be seen in the way that teaching and training has changed over the years. Three main approaches to learning include: behaviourism, cognitivism and the humanistic approach.

Table 3.1 The three main approaches to learning

Orientation	Characteristics	Considerations for tutors and trainers
Behaviourism	Learning is seen as a change in people's behaviour as a result of an action or experience. Behaviour can be determined through the environment and controlled through a 'stimulus-response' approach. The use of positive and negative reinforcements can lead to changes in behaviour.	Reinforcement of positive behaviour, for example through rewards or reinforcement of behaviour to be avoided, through sanctions and punishments. Learning through doing and practical activities allows for frequent practice and repetition – essential for learning to take place. Learning focuses on observable changes in behaviour, often highlighted through clear learning outcomes shared at the start of a session, for example: 'By the end of the session, learners will be able to …'.
Cognitivism	Concerned with what happens in the mind, learning is seen as a change in what we comprehend and how we develop new meaning. New learning builds on prior learning and what we already know. Learners seek insight by looking at the 'bigger picture' in order to try to make sense of the world.	Discussions, discovery and problem-solving tasks are activities that promote thinking, reasoning and understanding, to develop learners' insight and how they make meaning from new learning. The use of examples, case studies and metaphors is useful to build connections between old (prior) knowledge and new knowledge.
Humanistic	Learning from a humanistic perspective is concerned with human growth, the uniqueness of individuals. Learners are already programmed for growth and learning and to want to achieve their full potential. Learning involves the whole self, including feelings as well as cognitive processes.	Opportunities for learners to make choices about their own learning are important. A flexible approach to learning, where learners can exercise their own interests and satisfy their own needs is likely to be effective for the humanistic perspective. Activities that explore learners' own feelings, emotions and motivations may be useful in shaping effective learning experiences.

Situated learning

Situated learning theory lends itself to skills, knowledge and practices being learned within a particular context, for example the workplace. It also provides a context for real world learning and teaching, even if your sessions are delivered in simulation contexts, for example, in a workshop (plumbing) or salon (hairdressing and beautician). These settings can make the learning more meaningful as it relates to learners' real-life vocational aspirations. These shared goals and activities may be described as building a community of practice (Lave and Wenger, 1990) between you and your learners, which can be motivational and inspirational for all involved.

Theories of motivation

One of the best known theories relating to motivation comes from Maslow (1954) and his hierarchy of needs. Extensively used in the business and management world, the hierarchy of needs can highlight some important considerations for tutors when trying to engage and motivate vocational learners.

Figure 3.1 Maslow's (1954) hierarchy of needs (adapted)

Meeting individual needs

Aligned to the principles of the humanistic approach to learning, if learners' lower level deficit needs are well met, they are more likely to be motivated to learn and achieve. How can we try and meet these needs in vocational education and training?

We take for granted that our learners will have their physiological needs met before they arrive for learning. However, for many younger or vulnerable learners a good night's sleep, a filling breakfast and a clean uniform may not be a given. Some learners may have unsettled personal circumstances, financial problems or other priorities that prevent them from satisfying their basic physiological needs.

It is useful for us to be aware of scheduling appropriate breaks, ensuring our learning environments are well ventilated and of how to signpost learners to the relevant social support services. We need to know who our learners are and what their specific needs may be. The importance of robust and detailed initial assessment arrangements are key here and are explored further in Chapter 5.

Feeling safe, secure and welcome

Learners need to feel safe and secure in order to give their full attention to learning. Both physical and emotional safety is essential. In many vocational learning environments, risk assessments will need to be carried out to ensure the kitchen, the workshop, the garage or the dance studio are safe and fit for purpose. Risk assessments should follow your organisational procedure and identify hazards: who may be harmed and what needs to be done to reduce the risk to an acceptable level. Your learners should receive a comprehensive induction to staying safe in their vocational learning environments, including the safe and appropriate use of specialist equipment, chemicals or working with children or vulnerable adults for example.

The Health and Safety Executive (HSE, 2012) provides useful guidance on five key stages to risk assessment:

- Step 1: Identify the hazards.

- Step 2: Decide who might be harmed and how.

- Step 3: Evaluate the risks and decide on precautions.

- Step 4: Record your findings and implement them.

- Step 5: Review your assessment and update if necessary.

If learners do not feel emotionally safe, then their attention is unlikely to be focused on making good progress and achieving well. Creating a learning environment where both staff and learners are mutually respectful, where any forms of bullying or harassment are not tolerated and where all learners feel they are welcome is essential for engagement and maintaining motivation.

Equality and diversity is not about treating every learner the same. We need to know our learners well, identify and meet their specific needs and ensure that the rich diversity of our learners is celebrated and used to enhance learning. The Equality Act 2010 brought together many different pieces of equality legislation and includes key considerations for those working in education and training.

Table 3.2 Key considerations from the Equality Act 2010

Nine 'protected characteristics'	These are aspects of a person's identity explicitly protected from discrimination: • race; • disability; • gender; • age; • sexual orientation; • religion and belief; • gender reassignment; • pregnancy and maternity; • marriage and civil partnerships.

(Continued)

Table 3.2   (Continued)

Definitions of discrimination	The Act recognises the following types of discrimination: • direct discrimination, including association and perception discrimination; • indirect discrimination; • harassment; • victimisation; • discrimination arising from a disability; • failure to make reasonable adjustments.
Public Sector Equality Duty	Public sector organisations are required to work towards: • eliminating discrimination, harassment and victimisation; • advancing equality of opportunity; • fostering good relations.

As a tutor and practitioner, you need to ensure that your practice is inclusive and respectful, to ensure learners have equality of opportunity and that they feel safe to learn. Some of the ways you can do this include:

- **Carry out an equality analysis** – this considers the impact that your practice and the policies and procedures that you follow have on different individuals and their characteristics.

- **Evaluate your learning materials** – do your learning materials support or challenge key stereotypes in your vocational subject? For example, many learners attracted to childcare programmes will be female and, to construction programmes, male. Do your resources and promotional materials challenge these stereotypes and highlight positive role models who do not confirm to the 'majority'?

- **Reflect on the language that you use** – you need to ensure your language is inclusive and respectful to all learners. It is not sufficient to support discriminatory language or terminology which is 'commonplace' on the shop floor, salon, building site or sports pitch. As a vocational tutor, you are a role model who needs to reinforce and demonstrate appropriate language and terminology.

Activity

Examine your learning resources for a selected unit or module that you teach. Carry out an evaluation of the language and images used in your materials. Consider what messages they reinforce and if these support a diverse community and challenge stereotypes.

Consider the different types of learner that you teach. Do you know enough about their backgrounds and needs in order to understand how to plan learning that will meet their educational goals?

You may have identified a wide range of different 'learner types'. In the *Handbook for the inspection of Further Education and Skills* (2013: 40), Ofsted highlights the importance for tutors and practitioners of ensuring that all learners make progress and fulfil their potential, especially those whose needs, dispositions, aptitudes or circumstances may require particularly perceptive and expert teaching. It identifies a diverse range of learners that you may teach, depending on where you work. Learners may include:

- disabled learners, as defined by the Equality Act 2010, and those who have special educational needs;
- boys/men;
- girls/women;
- groups of learners whose prior attainment may be different from that of other groups;
- those who are academically more or less able;
- learners for whom English is an additional language;
- minority ethnic learners;
- Gypsy, Roma and Traveller learners;
- learners qualifying for a bursary scheme award;
- looked-after children;
- lesbian, gay and bisexual learners;
- transgender learners;
- young carers;
- learners from low-income backgrounds;
- older learners;
- learners of different religions and beliefs;
- ex-offenders;
- women returners;
- teenage mothers;
- other vulnerable groups.

Activity

Looking at the list of learners who may have different needs, dispositions, aptitudes or circumstances, consider what you would need to do to try to ensure all make progress and fulfil their potential. Do you have any support from elsewhere in your college, prison, charity, sixth-form centre or community centre to help you support and meet these diverse needs?

'That is so gay' is a phrase many tutors will hear when working with young people. The gay equality charity Stonewall (www.stonewall.org.uk) has produced a series of accessible and practical guides to help tutors have the confidence to challenge homophobic language in a way that is not time-consuming or difficult. Explore the guides and identify three ways that you could tackle and challenge the use of discriminatory language by your learners.

Anti-discriminatory approaches to learning and teaching: challenging stereotypes

Vocational education has historically been characterised by a high degree of gender segregation, for example health and social care, beauty therapy, travel and tourism, childcare and floristry are often seen as the domain of female learners. Motor vehicle studies, construction, engineering and information technology are traditionally seen as classically male occupations.

It is important that learners should have career choices that are not disregarded due to stereotyped expectations. Many learners however still opt for careers, and therefore learning choices, which reflect traditional gender roles because other options seem untenable. Better vocational guidance is needed to address this issue and for tutors to be more gender aware and thus more able to challenge stereotypes.

Activity

Is there a gender stereotype in your vocational subject? What do the statistics reveal about the gender split of learners in your organisation? How could you challenge vocational gender roles?

Extension Activity

Create a list of at least ten well-known individuals representing different career fields. Select individuals who may be considered to have a non-traditional career role based upon appearance (e.g. male beauticians or female bricklayers). It is best to have a variety of careers represented.

Examples of possible professions you could have represented on your list include:

- *politicians;*
- *bricklayers;*
- *nurses;*

- *police officers;*

- *chefs;*

- *builders;*

- *artists;*

- *business professionals;*

- *dancers;*

- *hairdressers;*

- *astronauts;*

- *secretaries;*

- *estate agents;*

- *stay at home parents;*

- *professors;*

- *travel agents;*

- *scientists;*

- *athletes.*

Once you have identified and listed these professionals, check newspapers, magazines or online sources, for example YouTube clips, for pictures representing each one. Number each individual and post the pictures, with corresponding number, on the walls throughout a classroom.

Once the learners have entered the classroom and found their seats, provide each learner with a sheet of paper that lists the different professionals posted throughout the room. Explain to the learners that they should:

1. walk around the room;

2. look at each picture;

3. try to determine which profession from their career list corresponds to which individual picture. After learners believe they have found a match, they should write the number found on the picture next to the profession on their career list.

Do not be surprised to find that almost every learner will have inaccurately matched a professional with the appropriate career. But this is the aim of the activity. Learners will be forced to make assumptions about certain professions based upon gendered messages they've learned regarding career choice and appearance.

Discussion: Once the activity is completed, give the learners the correct answers to match each profession. Then, lead a class discussion to process this activity. During this discussion, address important points such as: assumptions should not be made about an individual based upon appearances (for example hairstyles, tattoos, make-up etc.) and stereotypes. Possible questions for further exploration:

- Why did you assume that the young female is the nurse?

- Do you know any nurses that are not young females?

- What are some of the negative effects of stereotyping someone's profession based on appearance?

- Besides physical appearance, what are some other stereotypes you know regarding career choice (e.g. education level, geographic location, family structure etc.)?

- Do you know anyone who does not fit into these stereotypes?

It should be more apparent to the learners by the end of the discussion that stereotypes exist regarding different careers. But these stereotypes could hinder their career choice and exploration process if not addressed.

It is important for tutors to understand how people's perception of different occupations may be distorted because of learned stereotype beliefs regarding a given occupation. With this knowledge, tutors can discuss the consequences and negative impact these stereotypes can have on learners' career options. Such a discussion may encourage learners to consider professions they may have never previously considered, or at the least, expand upon already existing options.

Confidence and self-esteem

As discussed in Chapter 1, many of our vocational learners may have a history of low achievement, or exclusion and of dissatisfaction with a traditional, school-based education and general curriculum. Many learners may arrive at your college, pupil referral unit, short-stay school or training provider with very low confidence, a history of disruptive behaviour or no formal qualifications at all. It is the responsibility of all vocational tutors and practitioners to provide a good quality learning experience which develops confidence and self-esteem in order to be successful.

The use of positive reinforcements, rewards and 'extrinsic' motivators may be one way initially to improve motivation levels and confidence and to break the barriers associated with formal learning. Extrinsic motivators are those factors external to the learner that many encourage engagement and participation. Examples include:

Qualifications – getting a formally recognised certificate of achievement;

Employers – getting a wage or completing studies as part of an employment contract;

Parents – achieving and progressing well to impress parents, guardians or carers;

Peers – keeping up with or competing against friends;

Tutors – receiving praise and feedback from tutors and practitioners;

Money – grants and other incentives for attending or completing a course of study;

Rewards – other rewards, such as trips, visits, leaving early, events, sweets;

Sanctions – the avoidance of sanctions can be motivating for some, such as extra classes, 'detention', letters home, disciplinary warnings, removal of rewards and incentives.

The use of extrinsic motivators is aligned with a behaviourist approach to learning, where positive and negative reinforcement are seen as key to learning. However, research suggests that those learners who are more 'intrinsically' motivated, who learn for the enjoyment and interest in learning itself, are more successful overall. Research by Brooks *et al.* (1998) observes that while external rewards (extrinsic motivators) sustain productivity, they decrease interest in the task and therefore reduce the likelihood that the task will be continued in the future.

Activity

Consider the ways that you motivate your learners. Do you use extrinsic motivators – both rewards and sanctions?

How might you reduce the use of extrinsic motivators to develop learners' intrinsic motivation and desire to learn? List five actions that you might try.

Intrinsic motivation

According to humanistic theorists (for example, Carl Rogers) motivation might come from within an individual without any thought to the external reward. Learners obtain their own internal reward through an increase in self-esteem and sense of achievement when they reach their chosen goal. They may just feel the aspiration to succeed based on factors such as their own interest in an activity or the feeling of satisfaction that is achieved when they complete the necessary steps to achieve the chosen accomplishment.

This drive is called internal or intrinsic motivation, which means there are no outside forces (for example, the workplace) that influence whether an individual will ultimately achieve their goal. The fact that they do not attempt to achieve an external reward works toward the intrinsic value associated with the success of the target. Learners will be motivated to perform desired behaviours and neither punishment nor rewards are necessary to motivate the individual to succeed.

Duckworth (2013b) identifies that how tutors approach the issue of learner motivation, be it intrinsic or extrinsic, is determined, in part, by the andragogical (adult) or pedagogical (children and young people) philosophical underpinnings of the practitioners' teaching and learning strategies. However, she notes that the assumptions of andragogy can lead to unrealistic and idealistic expectations about the behaviour of adults. We would suggest that having an awareness of different approaches allows us to engage with learners in meaningful ways irrespective of their age. A meaningful way to address this is to view each individual and their needs as unique and to tailor a programme which may include aspects of what are considered andragogical and pedagogical models, a range of them both (and others) rather than the notion of one approach for adults and one for children and young people.

The key focus for practitioners therefore should be how to encourage our learners to develop an 'I **want** to learn' approach, an intrinsic passion for lifelong learning, rather than relying on the 'carrot and sticks' that tutors can provide to meet an 'I **need** to learn' approach. Vocational education and training can be very effective here as learners, often for the first time, see a real purpose and benefit to studying and learning. Developing an intrinsic motivation for learning links with 'self-determination theory' (SDT) proposed by Deci and Ryan (1985).

Their theory highlights the importance of competence, autonomy and relatedness to being intrinsically motivated. As vocational tutors, it is useful to consider how we can make learners feel that they are competent and getting it 'right', that they are in control of their learning and that they are part of a community of support.

Three factors that may help to enhance intrinsic motivation levels include:

1. **Feedback**: give process focus feedback which is frequent, specific, and immediate.

2. **Choice**: build in opportunities for learners to choose what and how they learn.

3. **Optimal challenge**: ensure learning is accessible but challenging; not too easy or unobtainable.

Creating a 'growth mindset'

The way that we provide feedback and praise can reinforce a growth or fixed mindset perspective in our learners. Over the last four decades, the research of Professor Carol Dweck (2006) has provided persuasive evidence that learners with 'growth mindsets' (a belief that abilities are fluid and changeable over time) are better learners than those with fixed mindsets (a belief that abilities are fixed and unlikely to change).

Learners with a growth mindset are more likely to seek out challenges, show greater persistence and resilience in the face of difficulties, learn from their mistakes and ultimately find themselves on the road to success and fulfilment of their learning potential. They focus on the 'mastery of learning' and are likely to have a strong intrinsic motivation for learning.

Learners with a fixed mindset have a view that their ability is fixed, genetic, that although you can learn new things, you can't really change how intelligent you are. Fixed mindset learners might have very set beliefs about subjects, topics and tasks they are just 'no good at'.

Table 3.3   Growth versus fixed mindset summary (Hymer, 2009)

Mindset:	Fixed	Growth
Your belief	Intelligence is a fixed trait	Intelligence is cultivated through learning
Your priority	Look smart, not thick	Become smarter, through learning

Mindset:	Fixed	Growth
You feel smart, when	Achieving easy, low effort successes and when outperforming others	Engaging fully with new tasks, exerting effort, stretching and applying skills
You avoid	Effort, difficulty, setbacks, higher-performing peers	Easy, previously mastered tasks

Feedback and how it can be used to cultivate a growth mindset is explored in more detail in Chapter 7 on vocational assessment.

Choice

Giving learners some choice in what, where and how they learn, where practically possible, may also help to raise motivation and to engage your vocational learners. If you are teaching on accredited programmes, you will have a set specification and assessment criteria to follow but there should still be opportunities for you to be flexible in your approach.

Consider how you design your curriculum, the order of the units you teach and the way you assess your learners. Are all these variables fixed or are you able to give your learners some choice and autonomy?

Vocational assessment is explored in more detail in Chapter 7 and we will unpick here how offering choice in assessment method may be one way to provide a level of autonomy in your approach that will appeal to learners.

Optimal challenge

If learning is too challenging or too easy, this is likely to lead to anxious, bored and unmotivated learners. Csikszentmihalyi's (2002) studies into 'flow' and the state of optimal concentration identify the need for a balance between how much we challenge our learners and their levels of existing skill. Too much challenge too soon may lead to high levels of anxiety, particularly if learners have a 'fixed mindset' approach to learning. Not enough challenge and learners are likely to feel bored and disengaged. This may lead to disruptive or distracting behaviour as learners look for other ways to keep stimulated.

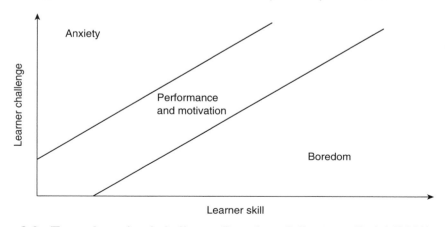

Figure 3.2 Towards optimal challenge. Based on Csikszentmihalyi (2002) 'Flow': The Psychology of Optimal Experience

Of course the optimal level of challenge will be different for each individual learner and this is arguably the vocational tutors' biggest challenge – how to differentiate learning to meet the needs of individual learners. By adapting and differentiating your approach to teaching, learning and assessment, you can attempt to create an environment of optimal challenge that will engage and motivate all your learners.

Ways to differentiate learning

- Differentiate your planning of learning, setting objectives that will be achievable by all, those achievable by some and those that you anticipate only a few will achieve in the first session. Good planning will help you to identify teaching and learning strategies that will stretch and challenge all learners given their individual starting points.

- Provide tasks and activities at a range of different levels – encourage your learners to choose their own level of activity which will challenge them to learn something new. Learners with a growth mindset should feel confident enough to attempt activities that are outside of their comfort zone and where they might be likely to fail.

- Use nominated questioning to ensure individual learners are sufficiently challenged based on their current level of skill and understanding. Questions that are 'open' and require more than a simple response are more likely to promote 'deeper' learning. Socratic or probing questioning can challenge your learners to think even more deeply and justify or expand on their initial responses.

- Encourage learners to ask each other questions based on their own learning. When considering posing a series of their own questions, learners need to review what they have learnt, evaluate the important aspects and consider how they might challenge each other.

- Provide opportunities for learners to extend their learning after the session, using materials on the virtual learning environment (VLE) or extension activities. Providing a range of multimedia resources online can provide valuable opportunities for learners to investigate further, to develop their independent learning skills and to carry out consolidation exercises.

Reflection point

How do you differentiate your approach to teaching, learning and assessment in order to provide each individual learner with the level of optimal challenge? Identify further ways that you can personalise the learning experience for all your learners.

Expectancy value theory

An approach developed by Fishbein (1975) highlights how learners' levels of motivation and subsequent behaviour are determined by how much they value the learning goal and how much they expect to be successful.

Motivation = expectancy x value

If your learners have low confidence, feel their ability is 'fixed' and they do not expect to be successful, then motivation to participate in learning and attempt learning tasks is likely to be low. If learners struggle to see the value of their learning, their course, their education, then their motivation to attend and participate is also likely to be low.

For tutors and practitioners, it is therefore important to highlight both the importance and value of vocational education and the likelihood that learners will be successful if they attend, participate and work hard.

The value of positive role models may well be useful in demonstrating the 'value' of learning. If learners can see and hear the positive results of working hard, of carrying out research, of completing coursework and taking exams, they are more likely to commit to their own studies and educational experience.

Attribution theory

Another theory that can help us to further understand behaviour and motivation is attribution theory. Heider (1958) was the first to propose a psychological theory of attribution. In Heider's view, people were like amateur scientists, trying to understand other people's behaviour by fixing together information until they arrived at a rational explanation or cause. Attribution theory focuses on how and why people explain events as they do. Therefore, it makes sense that the better we know someone, the more likely we are to attribute behaviour to the situation. According to Heider a person can make two attributions:

- **Internal attribution**: the suggestion that a person is behaving in a certain way because of something about the person, such as attitude, character or personality.

- **External attribution**: the suggestion that a person is behaving a certain way because of something about the situation she or he is in.

Attribution theory has been used to illuminate the difference in motivation between high and low achievers. According to attribution theory, high achievers will approach rather than avoid tasks related to succeeding, because they believe success is due to high effort, which they are confident of. Failure does not lower their self-esteem but success builds pride and confidence. They tend to continue when the work gets hard rather than giving up because failure is caused by a lack of effort, which they can alter by trying harder. They also tend to work with a lot of enthusiasm because the results are believed to be determined by how hard they try and the effort they put into the task. There are clear links here to a growth mindset approach to learning.

On the other hand, low achievers avoid success-related tasks because they tend to doubt their own ability and relate success to luck or to other influences outside their grip and so beyond their control. Therefore, even when successful, it is not as gratifying to the low achiever because they do not feel responsible; it does not increase their self-confidence and belief in their abilities.

Influence of a lack of motivation in a low achiever

Learners can switch off completely, or use a range of disruptive tactics to cover their lack of confidence. When learners underachieve, their ability and skills find no expression. This can result in their becoming disaffected, and they may well disturb others in the class. As we struggle to manage their challenging behaviour, our job satisfaction can lessen and in turn the morale of the class can be reduced.

Reflection point

Consider your current learners. Do any appear to be unmotivated? How do you know? What signs and signals do they show that lead you to think they are not motivated? What strategies could you try to get them motivated and switch back on to their studies? Do you think extrinsic or intrinsic motivators would be more effective? Do you feel they have a fixed or growth mindset?

Motivation through competition

Skills competitions can provide valuable and motivating opportunities for learners to apply their knowledge and understanding to a high standard. The Learning and Skills Improvement Service (LSIS, 2012) identifies a number of learning benefits for vocational learners who participate in competition activity:

- building stronger relationships with other learners;
- building collaboration between the tutor and the learner;
- identifying strengths and weaknesses;
- developing wider networks in other colleges and in industry;
- identifying a network of possible employers;
- improving commitment and reliability;
- improving problem-solving skills;
- gaining experience in associated and wider skills.

Competitions such as World Skills UK and World Skills International can provide a real motivating focus for many vocational learners. The chance to complete at the highest level with people from across the country, and the world, can be a very rewarding experience for many learners, along with improving their CV and ultimately their employability. Competition experience, whether at small internal events or on an international stage, can develop learners' wider skills of communication, independence and resilience. Skills competitions are explored further in Chapter 6 on experiential learning.

Promoting motivation

Learners will be more motivated to work if they know what goals they are working towards. A way to do this is by working together as opposed to the goals being tutor driven. This means utilising effective communication skills and placing the learners at the centre of their learning cycle. It is important to make the goals and the knowledge and skills that need to be developed through the goals explicit and meaningful.

It is a good idea not only to articulate goals for the course, but also personal goals. The two are likely to be closely linked and being aware of this is important to understand and respond to learners' motivations and hopes for the future.

Summary

In this chapter we have looked at a number of key themes:

- *the behaviourist, cognitivist and humanistic approaches to learning;*
- *theories of motivation and considerations for your practice;*
- *creating safe and secure learning environments through equality and diversity;*
- *differences between a fixed and a growth mindset;*
- *ways to differentiate your approach to learning;*
- *the importance of feedback, choice and optimal challenge for motivation.*

Theory focus

Further reading

Bloxham, S and Boyd, P (2007) *Developing Effective Assessment in Higher Education: A Practical Guide.* Berkshire: Open University Press.

Csikszentmihalyi, M (1990) *Flow: The Psychology of Optimal Experience.* New York: Harper Perennial.

Deci, E and Ryan, R (1985) *Intrinsic Motivation and Self-determination in Human Behaviour.* New York: Plenum.

Duckworth, V (2013) *How to be a Brilliant FE Teacher: A Practical Guide to Being Effective and Innovative.* London: Routledge.

Dweck, C (2012) *Mindset: How You Can Fulfil Your Potential.* London: Robinson Publishing.

Gould, J (2012) *Learning Theory and Classroom Practice in the Lifelong Learning Sector.* Exeter: Learning Matters.

Gravells, A and Simpson, S (2012) *Equality and Diversity in the Lifelong Learning Sector.* Exeter: Learning Matters.

Petty, G (2009) *Teaching Today: A Practical Guide* (Fourth Edition). Cheltenham: Nelson Thornes.

Swan, M, Peacock, A, Hart, S and Drummond, M J (2012) *Creating Learning Without Limits.* Maidenhead: Open University Press.

Tummons, J and Powell, S (2011) *Inclusive Practice in the Lifelong Learning Sector.* Exeter: Learning Matters.

Websites

Mindset: www.mindsetonline.com

Future First: www.futurefirst.org.uk

Ofsted: www.ofsted.gov.uk/resources/handbook-for-inspection-of-further-education-and-skills-september-2012

References

Bomia, L, Beluzo, L, Demeester, D, Elander, K, Johnson, M and Sheldon, B (1997) *The Impact of Teaching Strategies on Intrinsic Motivation*. Champaign, IL: ERIC Clearinghouse on Elementary and Early Childhood Education.

Brooks, S, Freiburger, S and Grotheer, D (1998) *Improving Elementary Student Engagement in the Learning Process Through Integrated Thematic Instruction*. Chicago, IL: Saint Xavier University (ERIC Document Reproduction).

Csikszentmihalyi, M (2002) *Flow: The Classic Work on How to Achieve Happiness*. London: Rider Books.

Deci, E and Ryan, R (1985) *Intrinsic Motivation and Self-determination in Human Behaviour*. New York: Plenum.

Duckworth, V (2013b) *How to be a Brilliant FE Teacher: A Practical Guide to Being Effective and Innovative*. London: Routledge.

Dweck, C S (2006) *Mindset: The New Psychology of Success*. New York: Random House.

Fishbein, M and Ajzen, I (1975) *Belief, Attitude, Intention and Behavior: An Introduction to Theory and Research*. Reading, MA: Addison-Wesley.

HSE (Health and Safety Executive) (2012) *Five Steps to Risk Assessment*. London: Health and Safety Executive.

Hymer, B (2009) *Gifted and Talented Pocketbook*. Alresford: Teachers' Pocketbooks.

JISC (2010) *Effective Practice with E-learning – A Good Practice Guide in Designing e-Learning*. Bristol: Joint Information Systems Committee.

Lave, J and Wenger, E (1991) *Situated Learning: Legitimate Peripheral Participating*. Cambridge: Cambridge University Press.

LSIS (2012) *Inspiring Excellence: A Guide to Embedding Skills Competition Activity in Apprenticeships and Vocational Learning*. Coventry: Learning and Skills Improvement Service.

Ofsted (2013) *Handbook for the Inspection of Further Education and Skills*. Manchester: Ofsted.

Maslow, A H (1954) *Motivation and Personality*. New York: Harper and Row.

In this chapter you will learn about:

- approaches to work with employers at different stages of the learning journey;
- the role of work experience in vocational learning;
- developing learners' functional, personal, learning and thinking skills;
- using social media to bring employers into the classroom.

Professional Standards

Standard 1: Identify collective learning and development needs – KU3 The types of stakeholders involved in an analysis of collective learning needs and why their support and commitment are important

Standard 5: Develop and prepare resources for learning and development – KU8 How to develop simulated exercises that replicate real working challenges

Introduction

In the previous chapters we have explored the importance and relevance of vocational study programmes which are clearly aligned to the needs of employers, considered the national occupational standards of the sector and made clear links to the development of skills and working competences required to be successful in the vocational industry of study. In this chapter, we explore ways to develop and reinforce the links with employers and how employment experiences can add a rich layer or realism and purpose to make education and training truly vocational.

Learning beyond the classroom

Today's vocational learners need learning experiences that go beyond the classroom and into the workplace, the salon and the workshop. Vocational courses can develop learning by helping learners:

- gain exposure to career options in industries they may not have known about or even considered;
- understand more about the industries both locally, nationally and internationally that they may want to pursue in the future;

- develop essential workplace skills;

- develop working competencies related to career aspirations;

- see how their in-class learning (for example, theoretical knowledge) can be applied in the workplace;

- make more informed decisions about their education and career paths so they make a successful transition into the job market.

The Department for Education (DfE, 2013) has signalled their commitment to the development of 'enterprise education' through new funding flexibilities for schools and colleges. There is now an expectation that schools and colleges will increase their engagement with employers and incorporate a range of enterprise activities that will complement the vocational qualifications and work experience that learners undertake as part of their study programme, as appropriate to the needs of the learners.

It identifies a range of examples for engaging with employers for enterprise, including:

- Enterprise projects – employers setting business briefs for learners to solve. This type of activity encourages team working, leadership, good communication, working to deadlines, problem-solving and requires an understanding of business finance.

- Mentoring – employers providing one-to-one encouragement and support to learners.

- Work shadowing – giving learners the opportunity to observe staff in real working environments.

- Workshops – employers leading discussions with learners on school, college or employer premises about the realities of work, and the employment and training environment.

In their report on excellent adult vocational teaching and learning, CAVTL (2012) highlights the importance of developing a two-way street approach to vocational education, one which gives vocational learners a clear line of sight to work. It identifies a spectrum of ways that the diverse range of vocational education provided can attempt to develop and maintain this two-way street:

- employer representation on groups responsible for the governance of vocational education and training;

- joint vocational course teams that are responsible for curriculum development, programme design, review and evaluation;

- wherever possible, ensuring that vocational programmes include a substantial, meaningful work placement;

- a range of other activities through which employers can contribute, including mentoring, running workshops, seminars, demonstrations, and through alumni networks;

- through local arrangements to encourage working people with vocational expertise to go into their local college or training provider and teach their trade or profession for a few hours a week;

- vocational tutors and trainers working in collaboration with employers on projects that add value to their organisations: developing new products, processes or markets, or providing technical support to small or start-up firms;

- joint investment in research and development centres, and leading-edge technology, to support the development and application of deep vocational knowledge and skills, and encourage entrepreneurial ambition.

Reflection point

Consider the range of ways that CAVTL suggest may provide opportunities for vocational education providers and employers to operate as a two-way street for the benefit of learners. Is your employer currently implementing any of the suggestions in its approach to vocational education?

As a dual professional, do you have access to continuing professional development in order to maintain your own vocational expertise, if you are now no longer a practitioner in the industry?

The use of vocational role models

Whether it's a successful former learner, a local entrepreneur or even a vocational professional working in an education environment (such as marketing, health and safety or human resources), the use of vocational role models can give learners a clear line of sight to the value of their vocational education.

With much awareness given to the value of higher education, it is crucial for vocational learners to hear about alternative routes to employment and financial success from vocational professionals who have followed both a vocational qualifications programme and a work-based learning progression route.

Case study

Supported by the Sutton Trust and a broad advisory council, Future First aims to provide each UK state school and college with an alumni-based model of careers advice. Future First hope to increase learners' social mobility, by linking former students with their old schools and colleges to support a range of learning opportunities, from role models, e-mentors, guest speaker visits and work placement opportunities.

Visit: www.futurefirst.org.uk

Activity

Consider the skills and expertise that you could contribute to learners at your former school or college. As a developing dual professional, identify the links, knowledge and experience that you could bring to the learning journey of young people. How can you integrate these links with your current learners and the subject you teach?

Learning during a work placement

With many employers increasingly looking for experience as well as qualifications in candidates for their positions, work placements have an increasing importance in gaining a good job. Regardless of how much you think the learners have learned about their vocational area from their studies they will learn so much information and acquire so many skills from a work placement. Learners can never really be on the ball with what a job entails until they have been working practically in that role.

If the vocational study programme is not work-based, such as a competence-based NVQ programme, then work placements offer the perfect opportunity to gain this kind of experience whilst still studying. An employer seeing any work placements on a learner's CV will be more likely to consider them for the position if it demonstrates the placements they have carried out.

Activity

Consider the vocational and wider skills that learners can gain from workplace experience.

You may have identified that they can gain:

- experience of teamwork and development of interpersonal skills;

- ability to work in a team and with colleagues around them – this is essential in every type of job; in a work environment this involves a different set of skills and challenges that they can utilise at school, college or university;

- chance of a firm offer of employment – performing well on a work placement may lead to a firm job offer at the end of it; even if a job offer is not possible, the contacts acquired and networking done during a placement will have put the learners in contact with people who may well be able to help them enter into and progress in their chosen career in the future.

What else is in it for your learners?

They will:

- start to understand how the skills they have learnt in the classroom relate to real working life;

- be able to apply those skills to a working situation;

- learn how to develop the skills employers look for in potential employees;

- develop valuable experience of working in teams with a range of different people at different levels;

- learn what employers expect from an employee and what the learners can expect from an employer.

You need to know what employers are looking for in order to support and prepare your learners for their work-based experience. Applied English language skills, functional mathematics and information and communication technology (ICT) skills are high on the list of skills that employers look for. Other desirable skills include:

- personal presentation;

- being reliable and punctual;

- being motivated and enthusiastic;

- an ability to behave in a professional way, for example, working positively with others at a range of different levels.

Personal learning and thinking skills (PLTS) were a set of transferable skills identified through the workforce and qualification reforms of the previous government and the development of the Diploma qualifications. Still a requirement for apprenticeship frameworks, PTLS can be useful to all vocational tutors in identifying a set of wider skills that may be developed through working with employers and in work placement experiences. For many learners, the development of PLTS may have the biggest impact on their employability.

The overall aim of the PLTS framework is to:

> [h]elp young people become successful learners, confident individuals and responsible citizens. The framework comprises six groups of skills that, together with the functional skills of English, mathematics and ICT, are essential to success in learning, life and work. (QCA, 2007)

The PLTS framework comprises six groups. The specification of apprenticeship standards (DFE, 2011), highlights what each learner needs to demonstrate in each of the six skills areas:

Table 4.1   Six skill areas for apprenticeship standards

1. Independent enquirers	Apprentices can process and evaluate information in their investigations, planning what to do and how to go about it. They take informed and well-reasoned decisions, recognising that others have different beliefs and attitudes.
2. Creative thinkers	Apprentices think creatively by generating and exploring ideas, making original connections. They try different ways to tackle a problem, working with others to find imaginative solutions and outcomes that are of value.
3. Reflective learners	Apprentices evaluate their strengths and limitations, setting themselves realistic goals with criteria for success. They monitor their own performance and progress, inviting feedback from others and making changes to further their learning.
4. Team workers	Apprentices work confidently with others, adapting to different contexts and taking responsibility for their own part. They listen to and take account of different views. They form collaborative relationships, resolving issues to reach agreed outcomes.
5. Self-managers	Apprentices organise themselves, showing personal responsibility, initiative, creativity and enterprise with a commitment to learning and self-improvement. They actively embrace change, responding positively to new priorities, coping with challenges and looking for opportunities.
6. Effective participants	Apprentices actively engage with issues that affect them and those around them. They play a full part in the life of their school, college, workplace or wider community by taking responsible action to bring improvements for others as well as themselves.

Involving employers at each stage of the learning journey can assist you in designing your study programmes to meet the demands of your vocational sector, to identify opportunities to embed functional English and maths and to develop learners' personal, learning and thinking skills.

Activity

Consider how you might actively engage employers in the design and implementation of your vocational study programme, whether a work-related, competency-based or more general non-accredited vocation course.

Course design

As the vocational tutor, you are likely to be involved with the planning of your own study programme. This might include designing a 'scheme of work' which plans out how a specific unit, module or whole programme will be delivered and assessed. Planning is explored in more detail in Chapter 5.

You might set up a local 'employer panel' and invite employer representatives from a range of sector-specific organisations. Each panel could meet regularly to assist you and your department in planning and designing your vocational programmes to reflect the current needs of the sector. The employer panel might review and advise on your course planning, making valuable contributions as to how employer-related skills could be further developed or enhanced. Panel members might also be suppliers of materials and resources. Attendance on the panel could help them meet their corporate social responsibility commitments.

When setting up an employer panel:

- Try to get representation from a range of local employers from different industries within your vocational sector.

- Encourage representation from public, private and voluntary sector organisations if possible.

- Invite local representatives from national or international companies to add a broader perspective.

- Gain support from your local Chamber of Commerce and Local Enterprise Partnership (LEP).

Teaching and learning

When working with your employer panel, or a range of local employer contacts, consider opportunities in your scheme of work where employers could make a valuable contribution to the teaching and learning of your vocational subject.

- Ask employers to come into the learning environment as guest speakers.

- Ask employers for copies of the forms, policies, procedures and paperwork they use (where appropriate) to add a level of realism to your class-based activities.

- Ask employers to be part of practical activities to present the view of the sector, for example sitting on interview panels for selection and recruitment role-plays or giving feedback on practical workshop sessions as learners apply their knowledge and understanding.

- Some employers might be prepared to give you access to some of their IT systems using test or practice accounts (so data protection is not compromised), to show learners how orders are processed, how details are recorded or how systems are automated to meet the needs of clients or customers.

Learning outside the classroom

Building a two-way street with your network of employers can give you access to rich and valuable learning experiences outside the classroom.

- Arrange visits to the premises of employers, take a tour, allow learners to speak with staff and watch employees at work. Learners might be allowed to take photographs or videos to enrich their evidence portfolios.

- Develop opportunities for on-site work placement, work experience or work shadowing.

- Employers might be prepared to act as mentors, meeting and working with learners on a one-to-one or small group basis on-site, to develop their skills and raise their aspirations.

Assessment and feedback

Your employer panel could help with the design of assessment activities and review your vocational assignment briefs to ensure they reflect scenarios that are realistic. The use of real forms and acting as expert witnesses can support practical assessment through observation, which is explored in more detail in Chapter 7.

Activity

Make a list of all the employers you currently have links with. Identify if you have areas that are not yet represented. Work with your departmental managers to set up an employer panel to work with you at each stage of the learning journey. Work with the panel to develop exciting, applied and experiential learning opportunities.

Employer case studies

If busy employers are unable or unwilling to visit your college or training provider or if insurance and health and safety prevent visits from taking place on their premises, employers may still be able to offer real-life case studies relating to their business and the people who work there.

Case studies can offer engaging opportunities for learners to apply their underpinning knowledge and understanding. Case studies do not have to be written but could make good use of multimedia to bring them to life.

Activity

The Times 100 Business Case Studies website provides tutors with a wide range of case studies based on high-profile international companies. Explore the website and identify one or two case studies which would be useful for your own vocational subject.

Visit: www.businesscasestudies.co.uk

Social media

It is easy to see how the explosion of social media has gripped many of our learners. For them, updating their Facebook status and Twitter feed is a key occupation! Social media is also very well used by the majority of medium and large employers and can be harnessed by tutors to bring employers into the learning environment remotely.

Table 4.2   Social media for vocational learners

Facebook www.facebook.com	The world's largest social networking site. Many employers use the power of Facebook's audience to communicate with their customers, posting updates about company news, offers and promotions.
Twitter http://twitter.com	The micro-blogging site allows businesses to update their followers in 140 characters of less. Subscribing to a range of vocational employers will give you and your learners access to a stream of sector updates, links and news.
LinkedIn www.linkedin.com	The professional social networking site, LinkedIn features the profiles and employment histories of many high-profile employees across virtually every employment sector. Explore the profiles of employees in high-profile organisations by sector, investigating their career path, progression routes and links to subject-specific groups.
YouTube www.youtube.com	An essential teaching tool for any vocational tutor, this video-sharing site offers a vast array of video resources from business and employers looking to show and share what they do. Bring the companies into your classroom or onto your VLE through the use of online video.
Pinterest www.pinterest.com	A content-sharing service that allows members to 'pin' images, videos and other objects to their pinboard. Many businesses have their own Pinterest board to share images, articles and news in a very visual way.

Activity

Get on line and explore the growing range of social media websites and applications (apps). Consider setting up your own vocational Twitter account for your subject and get your learners to 'follow you' on Twitter. 'Follow' ten employers in your specialist subject on Twitter and 're-tweet' the most relevant posts for your learners.

Case study

Jenny is a trainer in digital media production for an independent learning provider.

My career in television started in the mid 1980s when I left college with four O levels. There was no such thing as media studies back then. My careers advisor suggested I get some practical secretarial skills, so I completed a Pitman's Secretarial Diploma. The skills I learnt on that course became invaluable as my career progressed.

I gained my first job in the sector as an editorial assistant on the sports desk for breakfast television, and I quickly realised this was the profession I wanted a career in. I learned quickly; I had a love of sport and got to know the processes around television production. I quickly moved into a Production Assistant role for a high-profile news programme. While there, the editor suggested I should train as a journalist and producer, which I did and I didn't look back. Eighteen years later, I had won numerous awards for my hard-hitting documentaries, had travelled the world producing programmes with world leaders, dictators, sports personalities, showbiz and Hollywood stars.

During my time in the industry, I worked with a number of trainees – showing them the ropes and giving them a taste of what it was like to work in this dynamic but challenging sector. It wasn't until I was asked to contribute to a new education training programme that I realised there was a whole generation of young people who were fascinated by working in the media, but had no clue as to how that was going to happen. Many of these young people were not engaged by school and left without any formal qualifications to a life 'not in education, training or employment' – 'the NEETS'.

That was why in 2009 I left the media industry to create an organisation that would deliver vocational media skills to disadvantaged young people. I wanted to share my vocational experience and skills to help them prepare for an entry-level job in the industry. The industry is frustrating; it has to be the only industry in the world where you have an Oxbridge graduate, plus a young person with no qualifications going for the same job – with the same aspirations. As the media industry is so elitist and competitive, executives have the pick of the brightest, and the pushiest, young people. What chance do those with no formal qualifications or experience stand? However, the creative industries need people from all backgrounds and walks of life to keep delivering world-class quality digital content that serves the wider society.

As a vocational tutor, I have now worked with many young people who have dropped out of school or college. Some have been young offenders and care leavers and for many, their confidence has taken a pounding. Our learners get practically involved right from the start. We give them skills in digital video production, on how to use HD cameras, lighting, sound and desktop editing software. We develop their understanding of how to work as a team in order to create digital content, how to design web pages, to transform clips into video and how cloud computing can enhance group work.

They complete live media projects that really challenge them on a personal level. They see a relevance to learning and can relate to the tasks they are completing. This helps to keep them motivated and engaged. The tasks are challenging and this comes as a surprise to many. They all watch TV and most think being a presenter, or director, or interviewer is easy. They are all engaged in media all day; it's a major part of their life and identity.

The tutors are all industry professionals who have all worked for the large TV channels. Learners respect their experiences and backgrounds and know they are learning from those who have 'walked the walk'. They help the learners to acquire new skills quickly and we see their perception of what the media is about and what they themselves are capable of. They achieve a certificate to recognise their skills but it's also about raising their aspirations, developing their confidence and improving their wider social and communication skills. For me, this type of practical, vocational training is a vital route for those young people who have not excelled on academic courses.

Activity

What short course and enrichment opportunities are available for your own vocational subject? Are there local businesses that could give your learners access to industry professionals?

Case study

Alan is a lecturer in public services at a large further education college.

I served in the Army for 33 years before coming into FE two years ago. I served in the Infantry, starting my career as a Guardsman rising to the rank of Major by the end of my career. I have served all over the world including multiple operational tours of Northern Ireland, and a tour of Bosnia and Iraq.

I have instructed soldiers on several tours during my career including a two-year tour teaching Officers at the Royal Military Academy Sandhurst. The highlight of my career was receiving national recognition for my work in Iraq where I ran a team that trained an elite Iraqi police unit.

Public service teaching is a 'strange beast' as many of the learners want to join a uniformed public service but in reality will be unlikely to achieve this goal as the competition for jobs is so challenging. The course, although vocational in nature, is unlike hairdressing or motor vehicle studies, which have direct skills which lead to possible employment. The public service course has a broad spectrum of

(Continued)

(Continued)

subjects that will in some ways assist in securing employment but not just in a public service. The course makes learners better citizens as they operate in teams, have a more disciplined approach to work and are more confident by the end of the course. The way to teach the subjects on the course is to link units, where possible, to real situations in the public services so that you can bring it to life and show relevance.

This year I was given the lead for Unit 2: Teamwork and Leadership in the Uniformed Public Services. This has been a subject that learners have struggled with in the past, especially the assignment centred on team development theories. In the past it was completed as a written assignment with no direct links to a public service. I have changed the assessment method to a presentation and linked it to a real situation, which is a group of soldiers in training. This has been a resounding success with all the learners achieving either the Pass or Merit criteria. I have even had learners using theories in their humour in class, a major result!

My college has strong links to all the uniformed public services in the local area. The staff has over 135 years of service between them which is a key factor in bringing the subjects to life. Trips to public services are a vital element of the course, making the subjects 'real 'for the learners. They have spent a week with the Army doing low-level tactics, command tasks and communication exercises. During induction week all learners attend an activity day with the Army doing command tasks. This helps the groups to bond, but more importantly makes them realise that they are attempting to join a very different area of employment. The learners have also spent days with other armed forces and all the main emergency services.

This year I have also set up a six-week Territorial Army (TA) taster course. The main aim is to give learners a chance to experience a prolonged period of time with a public service with a view to future employment and a chance to join the TA whilst moving onto higher education, an aspiration many of them have.

Territorial Army Insight Course

Overview

The college, in conjunction with the local TA Regiment, will be conducting a six-week Territorial Army (TA) Insight Course based at the TA Centre. The course is open to all Level 3, second-year Uniformed Public Service learners.

Aim

The aims of the course are:

- to increase career opportunities of all participating learners;
- to broaden the learners' knowledge of the TA;
- to have a fun, engaging college experience;

- to receive a reference from a uniformed public service;

- to give learners a chance to volunteer, as the TA is a volunteer organisation.

Selection

Twenty-five learners will be able to attend the first course. Selection is based on attendance and achievement data and a selection interview. Only committed and dedicated learners need apply.

Course content

The course content includes:

- weapon training awareness;
- first aid;
- command tasks;
- camouflage and concealment;
- basic tactics;
- drill;
- shooting;
- map reading.

Summary

The course will give you an opportunity to experience life in the TA at first hand and will provide you with further evidence for Unit 2: Teamwork and Leadership and Unit 4: Discipline.

Teaching on the Uniformed Public Course is a very rewarding, fun occupation. The key to success is to keep the course real with as many links to the public services as possible. I would recommend that vocational tutors try to take their learners on as many trips as they can secure, as this keeps the learners engaged and broadens their horizons to other services that they may not have thought about. You must keep in the back of your mind as a lecturer that many of them will not achieve a career in a uniformed public service but what they learn on the course will make them more attractive to any future employer.

Activity

As an experienced former soldier, Alan is able to bring his subject to life and arrange vocational experiences with employers that provide real and engaging learning experiences. Consider your subject and your own links to employers and industry. What taster courses, trips, visits or guest speakers could you arrange to provide valuable opportunities to provide close-hand, personal experience of the subject?

Summary

In this chapter you learnt about:

- *approaches to work with employers at different stages of the learning journey;*

- *the role of work experience in vocational learning;*

- *developing learners' functional, personal, learning and thinking skills;*

- *using social media to bring employers into the classroom.*

Theory focus

Further reading

CAVTL (Commission on Adult Vocational Teaching and Learning) (2013) *It's about work... Excellent adult vocational teaching and learning.* London: Learning and Skills Improvement Service.

Coffield, F and Williamson, B (2011) *From Exam Factories to Communities of Discovery: The Democratic Route* (Bedford Way papers 38). London: IOE Publications.

Faraday, S, Overton, C and Cooper, S (2011) *Effective Teaching and Learning in Vocational Education.* London: LSN.

Institute for Learning (2013) *Leading Partnerships with Employers and Building Collaborative Professionalism: Towards Excellence in Vocational Education.*

Lucas, B, Spencer, E and Claxton, G (2012) *How to Teach Vocational Education: A Theory of Vocational Pedagogy.* London: City and Guilds Centre for Skills Development.

157 Group (2012) *Great Teaching and Learning.* www.157group.co.uk/files/great_teaching_and_learning.pdf

Websites

Times 100 Business Case Studies: www.businesscasestudies.co.uk

Local Enterprise Partnerships Network: www.lepnetwork.org.uk

Twitter: www.twitter.com

Facebook: www.facebook.com

Pinterest: www.pinterest.com

LinkedIn: www.linkedin.com

Future First: www.futurefirst.org.uk

References

DfE (2013) *Work Experience and Non-qualification Activity.* Available from: http://www.education. gov.uk/schools/teachingandlearning/qualifications/b00223495/post-16-work-exp-enterprise-educ (accessed 27 August 2013).

DfE/BIS (2011) *Specification of Apprenticeship Standards for England.* London: Department for Business, Innovation and Skills.

CAVTL (Commission on Adult Vocational Teaching and Learning) (2013) *It's About Work... Excellent Adult Vocational Teaching and Learning.* London: Learning and Skills Improvement Service.

QCA (2007) *A Framework of Personal, Learning and Thinking Skills.* Coventry: Qualifications and Curriculum Authority.

5 PLANNING YOUR APPROACH

In this chapter you will learn about:

- key considerations for planning vocational learning;
- the tools of session planning;
- models of teaching;
- the role of initial assessment and learning styles or preferences.

Professional Standards

Standard 1: Identify collective learning and development needs – KU4 The types of qualitative and quantitative information required to undertake an analysis of collective learning needs

Standard 2: Identify individuals' learning and development needs – KU13 Different methods of supporting learners to identify their preferred ways of learning, and how to use this information to support their learning

Standard 3: Plan and prepare learning and development programmes – KU1 How information acquired from analysing learning and development needs contributes to planning, and the factors that need to be taken into account

Standard 4: Plan and prepare specific learning and development opportunities – KU4 Factors to consider in selecting suitable delivery and facilitation methods

Standard 6: Manage learning and development in groups – KU10 How to co-ordinate learning and development activities to meet individual and group needs

Standard 7: Facilitate individual learning and development – KU13 How to assess and manage risk in own area of work whilst facilitating learning and development for individuals

Introduction

The importance of good planning should not be underestimated. Vocational study programmes in particular often demand more thorough planning than more general qualifications due to the diverse nature of the learning environments and the involvement of employers, as discussed in Chapter 4.

In this chapter, we explore different approaches to planning your vocational learning programme, the documents which might help you and some of the considerations necessary to design engaging, motivating and employment-focused teaching, learning and assessment opportunities.

Key planning considerations

When planning your vocational study programme and each individual session, it may be useful to consider a range of different factors, including:

- Who are you teaching, what are their needs and how you will know what these needs are?

- Where are you teaching, what facilities are available and what specialist resources will you have access to?

- How will you teach, what models and strategies will you use and how are these aligned to the demands of the specification?

- Which teaching skills will you use, what professional development do you need and what support is available to help you?

- What are the timescales involved, what are the key dates for induction, assessment and evaluation, and what timetable and holiday restrictions will shape your design of the learning programme?

- How will you engage with employers, and what trips, visits and guest speakers will you build into your programme to develop links with employers and provide opportunities for experiential learning?

- How will you engage and motivate your learners, ensuring they feel safe emotionally and physically and promoting a growth mindset in your approach?

- How will you ensure that learning is appropriately assessed for risk and that all the necessary steps are taken to reduce the hazards to both staff and learners?

- How will you assess your learners' progress and achievement, the application of their developing knowledge and understanding, and how will you record their skills competence?

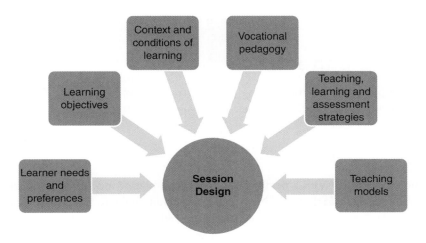

Figure 5.1   A framework for planning effective vocational sessions

Table 5.1 Exploring a framework for planning effective vocational sessions

Learner needs and preferences	Your sessions will need to meet the diverse needs of all your learners. Your planning should consider what these needs are and how you will meet them in each session, allowing every individual to make good progress through optimal challenge.
Learning objectives	For accredited qualifications, you will need to ensure the learning objectives for each unit or module are carefully considered, so learners are able to develop the knowledge, understanding and skills required to meet the assessment criteria.
Contexts and conditions of learning	Your learning environment may be a general use classroom but for many vocational subjects, it may take place with the support of specialist equipment, facilities and resources to bring your subject to life. The availability of resources will influence the way you plan your sessions and the activities you plan for learners.
Vocational pedagogy	How do you ensure that your session reflects the professional standards of the sector and maintains a clear line of sight to employers and enterprise? Ensure that your session planning identifies ways in which learning is experiential, links to the real world of work and provides opportunities for learners to engage with employers.
Teaching, learning and assessment strategies	Rather than just 'chalk and talk', excellent vocational teaching and training is likely to make use of a wide range of teaching, learning and assessment methods and strategies in order to engage and motivate learners.
Teaching models	You may find a particular pedagogical (or andragogical) approach helpful when structuring your session. A teaching model can give you a formal structure and sequence to follow to frame your approach to learning.

Planning paperwork

To help you plan, record and organise your approach to vocational learning, tutors are advised, and very often required by their employers, to create a variety of planning documents. These can include:

Scheme of work

A scheme of work (SOW) is a detailed plan of a whole unit or module of study and shows what will be covered each week. Many schemes include links to the learning outcomes (from the awarding organisation specification if accredited provision), key dates and timescales, including assessment points and links to the development of wider skills. For an example, see Appendix 1.

Case study

Catherine is a lecturer in business studies at a large further education college.

Vocational courses require learners to meet the set criteria. I see my role as finding as many different ways to help learners to achieve those criteria in ways that prepare them for real-life work. In business, recruiting is about getting the 'person', the technical skills will follow. Recruitment processes are largely shaped around the softer skills of innovation, perseverance, team work, time management and problem solving.

I believe the key to delivering vocational learning is not in the amount of content you cover. It is in the way teaching is planned, designed and delivered. Learning environments should encourage learners to explore new ideas and try out new ways of doing things and discover new opportunities. My schemes of work focus more on not what is to be covered each week, but how it is covered. For each unit I have the content to be covered coupled with 'how can I bring it to life' columns. This will involve guest speakers, real challenges such as working with the marketing team at the college, carrying out mystery shops at local retailers and presenting results back to them, and working on national business challenges.

Facilitation is the key. The more learners do themselves the more they develop these softer skills. It requires the tutor to be able to improvise, to keep being creative in their delivery, to take risks sometimes and to not be afraid to deviate from the plan. Most importantly, I make time to look for new opportunities, for example joining the local business network group.

As such the scheme of work typed up at the beginning of the year has to be flexible. It is scrawled all over with arrows where things have changed, been swapped around, been added. It includes sticky 'notes to self'. In a recent observation this was commended over the perfectly produced schemes usually presented.

Activity

Having read Catherine's approach to planning vocational learning, identify two actions that you could try to integrate into your approach to vocational teaching

Session plan

The session plan provides a detailed breakdown of the key tutor and learner activity for an individual lesson or workshop. A session plan will often include:

- the date and time of the session;
- the name of the tutor;
- the location of the session;

- the unit/ module details and the session topic;

- the key learning outcomes;

- timings;

- key tutor activity;

- what the learners will do;

- how the session is differentiated to meet individual learner needs;

- identification of opportunities to develop learners' functional English and mathematics skills and personal learning and thinking skills;

- key resources needed for the session;

- how learners will be stretched and challenged;

- how any in-session support will be best used to enable learners to meet the identified outcomes;

- considerations of any special circumstances and health and safety issues;

- formative and summative assessment strategies and methods;

- details of any directed study or homework to follow the session;

- signposts for the next session and linked content;

- an area to immediately reflect on action and action plan for the future.

From this comprehensive list, it is clear that a detailed lesson plan may take the less experienced tutor some time to complete. If you are teaching and training for 24 hours or more each week, creating a detailed plan for each session can become unmanageable.

Many tutors are beginning to adopt an approach where the scheme of work becomes the main planning tool, both for a full unit of study and for each individual session within the scheme. Whichever method of planning you adopt, the key is that the documents you create are useful to you and help you to plan meaningful and effective learning experiences that meet the needs of all your learners.

Group profile

In order to help plan learning to meet individual needs, many tutors find a class or group profile document a useful planning tool. Sometimes referred to as a 'cohort analysis', the profile form often includes initial and diagnostic assessment information for each learner in the group. This information may be useful in shaping your approach to teaching, learning and assessment, including your choice of teaching models and assessment strategies.

Typically, a group profile may include:

- learners' name (including their preferred name or self-selected 'nick-name'), age and gender;

- details of any prior learning or previous qualifications achieved;

- result of any initial assessments – for example English and mathematics assessments or a vocational skills assessment, such as an audition, interview or practical skills assessment;

- any identified learning differences or disabilities;

- any recorded allergies or specific needs;

- any other factors which affect their rate and level of learning.

Activity

Investigate your organisation's policy on planning learning and the templates that may be provided to structure and record your session planning. Does it provide a useful template to record all you need to in order to plan learning which meets individual needs?

Reflection point

Are you expected to complete a session plan for every session? Consider what you feel are the advantages and disadvantages of using a more detailed scheme of work as the main planning tool.

Health and safety

Recognising and addressing the role of health and safety in your planning is vital in vocational education. This can be carried out by:

- ensuring that the delivery of the vocational programme addresses health and safety in a clear and meaningful way;

- integrating health and safety messages into college-based and on-the-job training relating to key competencies for learners' chosen qualification and route;

- through induction by employers or supervisors prior to learners being allowed in a working environment;

- supporting college-based learning and employer inductions through the use of materials such as workbooks, guidance notes, internet webpages and DVDs;

- ensuring high-risk areas, such as workshops, performance spaces, laboratories, farms and environments involving animals, children, chemicals and tools receive additional and specialist risk assessment;

- ensuring all provider directed activities, such as off-site trips and visits, are subject to appropriate risk assessment processes and the relevant permissions are obtained.

Activity

What is the policy and procedure relating to ensuring the health and safety of both staff and students in your vocational area? Do you consider your vocational subject to be a 'high-risk' area? What steps do you take to reduce the risk of harm to your learners?

Teaching models

Models of teaching can be very useful when considering how to plan, sequence and structure your approach to a session. For many tutors in the further education and training sector, sessions can last as long as three hours and therefore require careful structuring to ensure they keep learners engaged and motivated.

Research by the Learning and Skills Network and City and Guilds Centre for Skills Development (Faraday *et al.* 2011) identified that many popular models of teaching are neither widely understood nor used in vocational teaching. They define teaching models as having two distinctive features:

1. **a defined sequence of steps or phases** that link to

2. **a type of learning objective and learning outcome**.

A simple teaching model might be to think of each session as a good meal, featuring set components which follow a particular sequence, for example:

Table 5.2   Components of a vocation session 'meal'

The starter	A learning taster which whets the learners' appetites for more.
The main course	The main body of learning where most of the learning takes place, either through information provided by the tutor or by learners working on activities to apply, experiment and consolidate their learning.
The dessert	The time to recap, summarise and check that learning has taken place. Set targets for next session.

Petty (2006) proposes the 'present, apply, review' (PAR) model of teaching as a way to structure a session.

Table 5.3   PAR model of teaching. Based on 'Structure for teaching a topic: the PAR model', from Geoff Petty (2006) *Evidence Based Teaching*

Present	Apply	Review
New material is presented, for example knowledge, reasoning, theories.	Learners work towards a challenging goal, for example problem solving, making decisions, creating things.	The learning is summarised and reviewed to explore if the goals and objectives were met.
Typical strategies could include PowerPoint presentations and giving demonstrations.	Learners will typically be engaged in a range of practical, experiential tasks.	Learning strategies could include note taking, discussion, reviews, quizzes and tests.

Educational psychologist Robert Gagne proposed a nine-stage theory of instructional design, which may be helpful to trainers in structuring their sessions:

1. Gain attention.

2. Inform learners of the objectives.

3. Recall prior learning (build on prior knowledge).

4. Present the stimulus (content).

5. Provide learning guidance.

6. Elicit performance (practice).

7. Provide feedback.

8. Assess performance.

9. Enhance retention and transfer (to the job).

Recognising and recording progress and achievement (RARPA)

For non-accredited programmes, such as more informal adult learning, which are not subject to the structures and requirements of a national qualifications framework, a structure of recognising and recording progress and achievement has been developed.

The application of RARPA promotes good practice in teaching and learning by placing learners at the centre of the learning process.

The RARPA staged process consists of five elements:

1. Aims: appropriate to an individual learner or groups of learners.

2. Initial assessment: to establish the learner's starting point.

3. Challenging learning objectives/outcomes: identification of appropriate objectives for the learner.

4. Formative assessment: recognition and recording of progress and achievement during programme.

5. Summative assessment: end-of-programme learner self-assessment; tutor review of overall progress and achievement.

Activity

Explore the RARPA toolkit, available from: www.niacedc.org.uk/rarpa-toolkit. How might you use the toolkit for structuring and planning your own learning programmes for non-accredited provision?

Activity

Consider a session that you are about to plan. Which teaching model would you find most useful and why? Do you feel the model you choose is dependent on what and who you are teaching?

Consider your own teaching model and the sequence of stages you feel are most appropriate.

Initial and diagnostic assessments

In order to plan vocational learning to meet individual needs, it is necessary to investigate what these needs are and to establish the learner's starting point. A range of tools, both electronic and paper-based, are used to gain information to help tutors carry out detailed and appropriate planning of learning to meet the needs identified. Initial assessment tools might include:

- application form;
- interview;
- audition;
- practical skills assessment;
- assessment of functional English language/literacy;
- assessment of functional mathematics/numeracy;
- free-writing exercise;
- analysis of learning styles and preferences.

Learning styles – friend or foe?

Much has been written about the use of learning style questionnaires as another tool in the initial assessment process. Many organisations routinely issue learning styles tools to try to identify the learning preferences and approaches of their learners in order to inform and influence the planning of teaching, learning and assessment.

One of the most popular frameworks of learning styles is the Visual Auditory Kinaesthetic (VAK) or VARK model (Fleming, 2001). This model suggests that learners may have a stronger preference (not necessarily strength) for approaching and assimilating their learning if it is delivered and presented in a particular way – for example, those who prefer to learn visually through diagrams, illustrations and visual models; those who appear to gain knowledge and develop an understanding through listening, delivered through tutor talk, discussions and audio recording; or those who have a kinaesthetic learning preference, achieved through learning by experience, practical hands-on approaches, experiential tasks and activities.

Activity

Complete your own VAK tool to identify what your own 'learning preference' might indicate. Visit: www.vark-learn.com

What do you feel are the advantages and disadvantages of using such tools with your own learners?

The popularity of accessible learning style tools has swept the FE and Skills sector particularly, but serious caution should be noted by all tutors and practitioners. It becomes easy to 'label' learners and their 'learning styles' but this can have serious consequences for the mindset of learners and the teaching methods of tutors.

Basic questionnaires completed over a few minutes, on one single occasion, arguably provide little valuable and reliable information on how to tailor approaches to learning. Even if this were possible, it is our responsibility as tutors to prepare our learners to be flexible, adaptable and resourceful enough to deal with a variety of learning experiences and approaches. The world of work and higher education will not be presented in one particular style, so it is our responsibility to develop learners' strategies and approaches through a variety of methods, modes and media.

Extension Activity

Read the Coffield et al. (2004) report which analyses a range of learning style tools and their reliability and validity.

What recommendations does the report propose for tutors and what does this mean for your own practice in planning teaching, learning and assessment?

Visit: http://itslifejimbutnotasweknowit.org.uk/files/LSRC_LearningStyles.pdf

Coffield *et al.*'s (2004) critique of different learning style tools highlights the different schools of thought and range of theoretical models of how people learn. Honey and Mumford (1982) identify four different preferences, or ways in which people prefer to learn, each related to a different stage of the learning cycle. These preferred learning styles they call: Activist, Reflector, Theorist and Pragmatist. Some learners may be most comfortable operating in just one 'mode', others in two or even three. The model is often used in business, leadership and management but raises considerations for the vocational practitioner.

Activists

Activists quickly involve themselves in new experiences. They enjoy the here and now and are happy to be dominated by immediate experiences. Their philosophy is 'I will try anything once'. They are always looking for new approaches/experiences. They learn least well from passive situations like reading, watching or listening to lectures. They do not enjoy solitary work, repetitive tasks, situations which require detailed preparation, or being asked to review their learning opportunities and achievements.

Activity

Consider how your subject specialism lends itself to an activist approach.

Reflectors

Reflectors like to watch, ponder and stand back whilst they consider the different perspectives. They collect data, both first-hand and from others, and prefer to analyse them thoroughly and think about them from every possible perspective prior to arriving at any definite conclusions. These they delay as long as possible. Indeed, their philosophical outlook is one of caution. They enjoy watching other people in action and prefer to take a back seat in lessons, for example role-play and discussions. They think before they speak. They tend to adopt a low profile and have a slightly distant, tolerant, unruffled air about them.

Reflectors learn best from activities where they are able to stand back, listen and observe. They like to have a chance to collect information and be given time to think about it before offering an opinion or acting. They like to evaluate what has happened. Reflectors learn least well when they are rushed into things with insufficient information or without time to plan, when they are forced onto the centre stage by being required to role-play or lead a discussion.

Activity

Consider how your subject specialism lends itself to a reflective approach.

Theorists

Theorists like to analyse and synthesise. They assimilate and convert contrasting facts and observations into coherent, logical theories. Their philosophy enjoys rationality and logic above all. They think problems through in a logical, step-by-step way. They tend to be perfectionists who will not rest easy until things are in a logical order. They are keen on basic assumptions, principles, theories, models and systems thinking. They tend to be detached, analytical and dedicated to rational objectivity. They feel uncomfortable with subjective judgements, ambiguity and lateral thinking.

Theorists learn best when they are offered a system, model, concept or theory, even when the application is not clear and the ideas may be distant from current reality. They like to work in structured situations with a clear purpose, and be allowed to explore associations and inter-relationships, to question assumptions and logic and to analyse reasons and to generalise. They do not learn well when faced with activities lacking depth, when resources and information are unavailable. They really enjoy being challenged intellectually.

Activity

Consider how your subject specialism lends itself to a theorist approach.

Pragmatists

Pragmatists are eager to partake in new ideas, theories and techniques to see if they work in practice. They are the sort of learners who after lessons are bursting with new ideas which they want to try out in their specialist area. They like to get on with things, and act quickly and confidently on ideas which attract them. They tend to be impatient with ruminating and open-ended discussions. They are essentially practical, down-to-earth people, who like making practical decisions and solving problems.

Pragmatists learn best when there is an obvious link between the subject matter and their specialist area. They like being exposed to techniques or processes which are clearly practical, have immediate relevance and which they are likely to have the opportunity to implement. Pragmatists learn least well where there are no immediate benefits or rewards from the activity and the learning events are not related to their situation/subject specialism.

Activity

Consider how your subject specialism lends itself to a pragmatist approach.

For more information, visit: www.peterhoney.com

Mindset analysis

We explored in Chapter 3 the work of Professor Carol Dweck (2006) and her research that learners with 'growth mindsets' are more likely to seek out challenges, show greater persistence and resilience in the face of difficulties, learn from their mistakes and ultimately find themselves on the road to success and fulfilment of their learning potential than those with a 'fixed mindset'.

As part of your initial assessment of learners during induction, we would support an investigation of learners' mindset to inform planning of learning for the group, which reinforces an approach where intelligence and ability is not seen as fixed but one where hard work, effort and optimal challenge can lead to high levels of success.

Name: _____   Tutor: _____

Course: _____   Group: _____

Implicit theories of intelligence scale – self form

Read each sentence below and then circle the one number that shows how much you agree with it.

There are no right or wrong answers.

*1. You have a certain amount of intelligence, and you really can't do much to change it.

1	2	3	4	5	6
Strongly Agree	Agree	Mostly Agree	Mostly Disagree	Disagree	Strongly Disagree

*2. Your intelligence is something about you that you can't change very much.

1	2	3	4	5	6
Strongly Agree	Agree	Mostly Agree	Mostly Disagree	Disagree	Strongly Disagree

*3. You can learn new things, but you can't really change your basic intelligence.

1	2	3	4	5	6
Strongly Agree	Agree	Mostly Agree	Mostly Disagree	Disagree	Strongly Disagree

4. No matter who you are, you can change your intelligence a lot.

1	2	3	4	5	6
Strongly Agree	Agree	Mostly Agree	Mostly Disagree	Disagree	Strongly Disagree

5. You can always greatly change how intelligent you are.

1	2	3	4	5	6
Strongly Agree	Agree	Mostly Agree	Mostly Disagree	Disagree	Strongly Disagree

6. No matter how much intelligence you have, you can always change it quite a bit.

1	2	3	4	5	6
Strongly Agree	Agree	Mostly Agree	Mostly Disagree	Disagree	Strongly Disagree

Scoring

Add up the scores from the first three statements (3 x 6 = total out of 18) then divide by 3 to give average score out of 6. The scores from statements 4–6 are discarded. Score of 1–3 is fixed mindset, 4–6 is growth mindset indication of a class, i.e. the percentage of fixed and growth mindset learners, but reliability for individuals is relatively low.

Figure 5.2   Mindset student questionnaire adapted from Dweck (2006)

Activity

Take the mindset assessment yourself and then explore the mindset website and the steps that can be taken to change a fixed mindset to a growth one. How might you use the concept of mindset with your own learners to help them fulfil their learning potential?

Visit: www.mindsetonline.com

Developing learners' literacies

Research from the Teaching and Learning Research Programme (2008) highlighted that 'literacy is a significant factor affecting retention, progression and achievement in colleges'. The study identified how the span of literacy practices in college, for example, reading resources and writing notes, was less than that which the learners engaged in in their everyday life, for example using measurements to work out how much wallpaper is needed to decorate a room, writing poetry, using social networking sites and applications like Facebook and Twitter to communicate with friends.

As tutors we can recognise and value the literacy approaches learners use across their life by adopting a 'social approach' to literacy, which is sometimes grouped under the term of the 'New Literacy Studies' (for more information see the work of Barton and Hamilton, 1998; Gee, 1996 and Street, 1984). It is generally thought that recognising the literacies that learners bring into the classroom is an effective strategy for teaching and learning because purposeful and meaningful learning builds and expands on learners' prior knowledge and experience. This learning helps to shape and construct new knowledge based on their prior experience and 'life', rather than seeing the learner as an empty vessel ready to be filled with facts and knowledge by the tutor.

It also recognises how literacy practices vary from one cultural and historical context to another. Many of your learners may come from very different cultural backgrounds. The social literacy practices of your younger learners may well be different from adult learners. Importantly, as well as literacy education being a key factor of vocational learning it has also been shown to enhance confidence, contribute to personal development, and promote health and social and political participation. When planning your vocational study programme, it is important to consider how you will also develop your learners' literacies.

Activity

Consider how a social approach to literacy can be used to help you plan an effective vocational curriculum.

Duckworth (2013a) identifies a number of ways that you might develop literacies through vocational programmes, including:

- Consider 'learning cultures' that build trust, honour diversity and develop confident learners.

- Recognise the diverse literacy practices learners bring into the classroom, workshop or salon and utilise them in the session.

- Use assessment methods that consider the readiness of learners, emphasise formative assessment and include assessment of soft outcomes.

- Use modern technologies to make literacy relevant to learners' everyday working and social lives, as well as promoting digital literacies.

The teaching and learning resources you use could be developed by, or in partnership with, your learners to capture and give meaning to their experience, motivation and aspirations.

Vocational literacies

When initially assessing your learners to help with your planning, you might also consider how much of the vocational terminology and 'jargon' your learners know. This will help you to plan activities that may be needed to introduce learners to the specific 'lexicon' of your vocational domain.

Table 5.4 Examples of vocational and specialist terminology

Hairdressing	Accent colour
	Acid mantle
	Hair integration
	Outer root sheath
	Vellus
Plumbing	Air gap
	Backsiphonage
	Flushometer valve
	Interceptor
	Leaky faucet
Bricklaying	Cavity
	Gauge
	Levelling
	Mortar
	Stretcher bond
Chef	Barding
	Concassé
	Deglaze
	Dredge
	Sous chef
Business	Horizontal integration
	Liabilities
	Netiquette
	Psychographic segmentation
	Remittance advice slip
Art and design	Approximate symmetry
	Amorphous
	Biomorphic shapes
	Neo-romanticism
	Primer
Health and social care	Anaemia
	Bradycardia
	Diabetes mellitus
	Hypertension
	Hypoxia
Equine studies	Bell boot
	Cinch
	Dressage
	Fetlock
	Hinny

(Continued)

Table 5.4   (Continued)

Travel and tourism	Pax
	Carrier
	Fam trips
	Hub
	Tariff
	Staged authenticity
Computing	Encryption
	Ergonomics
	Lossy
	Passive-matrix
	Winsock
	Defrag
Childcare and early years	Attachment
	Developmental milestone
	Gross motor development
	Respite
	Weaning
Drama	Antagonist
	Connotation
	Dramatis personae
	Monologue
	Villanelle

Activity

What specialist jargon and language does your own vocational area have? Make a list of all the terms that you can think of. Now complete a glossary of what each term means and make this available to your learners in a learner handbook or via the VLE.

Functional skills

Functional skills relate to a learners' ability to use applied English language, mathematics and ICT. Many learners in the UK struggle to achieve a functional level of literacy and numeracy and this can impact on their employability and how well they can make progress in their vocational qualifications.

The majority of learners on funded, accredited programmes will also be required to demonstrate a set level of competence in functional skills. This level of competence is usually assessed through a formal assessment and examination, often taken through an on-screen, on-demand test or through a traditional written-style examination paper.

It is important for the vocational tutor to have a good understanding of their learners' level of mathematic and English skill as this may well impact on the planning of learning and the range and type of learning tools and strategies used. Many vocational learners have good practical skills but can often struggle when it comes to writing, recording and reflecting on their learning through writing assignments, logs and journals.

Activity

Investigate what arrangements your learning provider has in place for carrying out initial and diagnostic assessment of learners' functional and applied skills in English language, mathematics and ICT.

Extension Activity

Explore the specific functional skills criteria for English, maths and ICT at the most appropriate level for your learners. Many learners working towards a vocational programme at Level 3 may be working towards their Functional Skills qualifications at Level 2.

Identify which skills might be developed through the tasks and activities you have planned for learners in their vocational sessions.

Visit: www2.ofqual.gov.uk/downloads/category/68-functional-skills-subject-criteria

All vocational tutors have a responsibility to develop learners' skills in functional English and maths and to find creative and engaging ways to contextualise and embed these skills in work-related contexts. This is a contentious strategy however, with many vocational tutors poorly equipped and qualified to deliver these core skills.

Reflection point

How do you rate your own English, maths and ICT skills? Are your own spelling, punctuation and grammar (SPaG) skills up to scratch to allow you to develop these functional skills with your own learners?

What about your own digital literacy skills? Are you able to develop the skills of your learners, who themselves have grown up in a digital, knowledge age?

As well as functional English and maths, we would argue that learners' digital literacy skills should also be a key focus of development for all tutors and practitioners working in the FE and Skills sector.

Digital literacies

In a digital age, learners need to practise and experiment with different ways of enacting their identities, and adopt subject positions thorough different social technologies and media. These opportunities can only be supported by academic staff who are themselves engaged in digital practices and questioning their own relationships with knowledge. (Beetham and Oliver, 2010: 167).

In today's digital, knowledge age, it is becoming ever more crucial for learners to have good digital skills to help them with online research, to use and navigate online systems such as the VLE and their e-Portfolios, and take part in online assessments, for example.

Part of the vocational tutor's role is not only to identify opportunities to embed and develop functional English and mathematics skills through vocational teaching but also to develop learners' own digital literacies.

Case study

John is a lecturer at a higher education centre with a further education college.

I worked in the construction industry for over 20 years, many as a senior manager working with large teams on site. After taking a part-time PGCE qualification at my local college (in partnership with a university), I gained some teaching hours at the college teaching lower-level learners on BTEC Construction courses. Funding became difficult and many of my groups were merged together or courses rationalised.

I then moved to teaching higher education in further education (HE in FE) at a local college HE centre. My learners are typically Higher National Diploma (HND) or degree undergraduates. The courses I teach are at Levels 4 and 5 of the qualifications framework and each module specification is mapped to professional education standards such as those from the Chartered Institute of Building (CIOB). The courses I teach are designed to prepare learners for working in the construction sector at a professional level.

I use my practical sector management experience and my teacher training to get the message across. I feel that my vocational experience gives me credibility in the classroom. My learners also work in the industry and they know the realities of the day-to-day pressures of working in the industry. Because I also come from this background, I am able to highlight how the theory links with the day-to-day practice in the 'real world'. I still plan my lessons in detail. I know other colleagues teaching higher education courses who do little formal session planning but I find it is very important to consider the different aspects of the session and how best to use the time to greatest effect. I use a session plan template, consider the 'Present', 'Apply' and 'Review' stages and ensure I leave time for discussion and questions.

I try to use technology in my approach to the session. I find there are a lot of relevant clips on sites like YouTube. This is also a good way of keeping up to date, exploring recent stories and articles in the news relating to construction and design technology. Learners like to be able to apply what they are learning through the use of case studies and group projects. As they are preparing to work as senior managers, I try to develop their wider skills through preparing and delivering presentations and participating in peer review and evaluation tasks.

At the higher levels, the sessions I teach now are less 'hands-on' than other vocational courses such as brickwork or joinery. For this reason I tend to find that seminar-type sessions work best for what we need to deliver. I am able to share my years of experience as a manager and senior manager. Learners are also able to share their relevant experience to date. At this level, the learners are encouraged to be more autonomous, sharing sources of independently acquired knowledge. I set them research and discussion tasks and find that this helps them acquire new knowledge and a better understanding.

Activity

Examine John's session plan example and identify how his approach to planning learning incorporates initial assessment and teaching models.

University Centre – School of Construction and the Built Environment Session Plan		
Staff Name:	**Date:**	**Lesson:** 6
Course: HND Construction Yr2	**Level:** Year 2 (F/T) – Level 5	
Subject: Design technology		
Session Aim: To identify and predict the mechanisms by which construction materials or components fail.		
Objectives: By the end of the lesson learners will be able to: • identify and explain at least three causes of failures of construction materials or components (Module specification LO ST200005.1/2).		
Opportunities within the session for developing and practising Functional Skills: Maths/Numeracy – dimensions of materials, components and fixings where appropriate. English/Literacy – discussion and presentation of individual ideas, note taking and annotation of sketches. ICT – use of interactive board and Moodle VLE.		

Figure 5.3   A vocational session plan example: construction   *(Continued)*

Figure 5.3 (Continued)

Time	Learning Phase	Learner Activity	Differentiation	Resources/ use of ILT
5 mins	Preparing learners for learning. Welcome and registration. Tutor identifies and shares this session's learning outcome.	Learners prepare to commence session. Consideration of outcomes. Clarify any questions.	Differentiated questioning as appropriate.	Interactive board
15 mins R	LO ST20005.1 Tutor instructs learners to complete 'puzzlemaker' formative assessment to recall the learning from the last teaching session – '**establishing quality management systems**'.	Learners complete puzzle. Learners share ideas with peers.	Learners who attend on time and those requiring less support complete the exercise more quickly – extension activity available. Those who do not complete the exercise can complete the answers during the review.	Puzzlemaker Pens and paper
5 mins R	LO ST20005.1 Tutor invites learners (sometimes nominated) to present their answers to the puzzle to the group.	Learners contribute to confirming the correct answers.	Check participation and accuracy of answers from individuals.	Puzzlemaker Pens and paper
10 Mins P	LO ST20005.2 Tutor introduces learners to new topic – failure mechanisms. Tutor identifies videos on Moodle, shows the videos, and then invites comments.	Learners observe videos, make notes to address scaffold questions and comment.	All learners are able to comment on building failures. Some learners are able to link with learning from other modules.	Interactive board Moodle
25 mins P	LO ST20005.2 Presentation – tutor, with reference to PowerPoint slides, opens a seminar discussion concerning identification of failure mechanisms in buildings. Tutor advises that the PowerPoint presentation is uploaded to Moodle. Tutor uses appropriate anecdotes associated with industrial experience. Tutor raises open and nominated questions concerning the subject content.	Learners listen, discuss and take notes. Invited to ask and answer questions throughout to check learning. Stretch and challenge – learners invited to share their own experience as relative to the topic, linking theory and practice.	Level of learners' questioning and answering. Different levels of note-taking skills. Resource on Moodle for those requiring support.	Whiteboard Pen and paper Computer and projector PowerPoint slides Moodle VLE

Figure 5.3   (Continued)

Time	Learning Phase	Learner Activity	Differentiation	Resources/ use of ILT
15 mins	Break			
20 mins P	LO1 ST20005.2 Tutor issues handouts to support discussion – 'life expectancy of components'. Tutor raises open and nominated questions concerning the subject content.	Learners listen, discuss and take notes. Learners complete handout tasks in small groups, drawing on prior knowledge and new knowledge. Learners ask questions.	Level of learners' questioning and answering. Differentiated task questions for different groups – stretch and challenge for group A. Level of responses to questions.	Handouts Whiteboard Pen and paper
20 mins A	LO1 ST20005.2 Tutor invites the cohort to consider how they will **apply** the new knowledge concerning cracking and movement of buildings.	Learners initially discuss and prepare short verbal presentation concerning failure mechanisms of buildings, implications for practice and relevance to summative assignment. Learners invited to peer evaluate each group's ideas and presentation style/ technique.	Mixed ability discussion/ presentation groups. Application to personal work contexts.	Paper and pens Whiteboard
15 mins R	Checking/assessment of learning. Tutor reviews learning which has taken place. Tutor raises open and nominated questions requiring learners to identify and explain at least three causes of failure in buildings.	Learners discuss their findings with the other members of the cohort. Completion of summary quiz.	Quality of discussions. Eagerness to share learners' knowledge with others. Level and accuracy of comments. Check on individual performance in summary quiz. Target support as required.	Whiteboard and pens Paper and pens
10 mins R	Tutor requests learners to complete a session feedback questionnaire.	Learners complete the questionnaire.		Questionnaire Pens

Session plan				
Course: VRQ Level 2 Certificate in Cutting Women's Hair				
Topic: Practical/commercial salon				

Date:		Time: 6–9 pm	No. on register:	12	**Additional learning support requirements**
Room:		Duration: 3 hours	No. present:		What are the specific requirements of the learners on this course? All individual support plans have been addressed and documented and are visible in the course file under each individual's name.

Safeguarding and risk assessment:	**Links to Functional Skills:**
A risk assessment is in place and is updated annually. All rooming and resources are checked before class to ensure all equipment is in safe working order. Learners are aware of their rights, roles and responsibilities via tutorial system. Learners are aware of class values and their behavioural expectations. Learners have participated in health and safety training during induction. Tutors and learners to conduct visual risk assessments each session. Appropriate health, safety and hygiene practices to be observed at all times. Products used in this session have been risk assessed and quality assured. Personal protective equipment (PPE) provided as necessary.	**Functional English (FE)** • Following verbal and written instructions and active listening. • Make a range of contributions in discussions. • Producing written expectations/evaluations for performances in session. • Giving and receiving verbal feedback and instructions. • Make effective consultations with clients while presenting a range of visual aids. **ICT** • Use ICT systems to convert digital images into photographic evidence of services. • Use ICT to access 'www.myhairdresser.com' for extension/research activities. **Functional Maths (FM)** • Calculating the cost of a client's service.
Personal Learning and Thinking Skills	• Identifying timescales /deadlines.
Independent Enquirer = **IE** Creative Thinker = **CT** Team Worker = **TW** Self Manager = **SM** Reflective Learner = **RL** Effective Participant = **EP**	• Calculating and drawing angles when cutting.

Equality and diversity	**Resources**	**Meeting individual needs**
Detail how the activities planned in the scheme link to the E&D agenda. • Teaching and assessment methods incorporate preferred modes of learning to aid progression and achievement. • Differentiated extension activities for learners need to stretch, challenge and enrich where necessary.	• Course file • Register (paper/ electronically) • Appointment sheets and client record cards • Consultation sheets • Practical task activity sheet • Hairdressing kit • PPE	• Using e-learning to offer the learner more exciting and innovative tools for active learning, enabling the learner to research, collaborate and create. • Tutor will break down tasks allowing the learner to scaffold their learning and become more independent.

Figure 5.4 A vocational session plan example: hairdressing

Figure 5.4 (Continued)

• Differentiated questioning to confirm learning and understanding and scaffold learning. • Learners to receive direction on how to deal with clients with disabilities as required. • Learners to receive insight into cutting men's hair to enable a unisex salon environment. • Clear direction will be given from the tutor to learners to ensure no culture or ethnic background is discriminated against when dealing with clients' requests. • Learners will develop skills in identifying relevant ethnic hair types. • Tutor will ensure that the learning environment is conducive to learning and the layout is accessible to all learners and clients. • Tutor will use appropriate inclusive, sensitive language and will challenge inappropriate language, prejudice and stereotyping.	• Head blocks • All available salon resources/tools and equipment. • E-learning: www. myhairdresser.com • Flip chart • Whiteboard markers • Sticky notes	• Assessment for learning will involve checking learning and giving constructive feedback so the learner can identify and focus on their efforts. • Previous commercial tracking sheets and data are used to identify progress to date to enable individual target setting in the session and allocation of clients.

Session aims	**Learning outcomes**
1. To provide learners with an opportunity to build confidence and practise skills for: shampooing, styling, cutting. 2. To provide learners with an opportunity for formative and or summative assessments on skills to date to VRQ Level 2 standards. 3. To reinforce and scaffold previous knowledge gained on skills to date. 4. To allow the learner an opportunity to self/peer reflect and evaluate performance within the session.	**All learners will be able to:** 1. Identify client requirements through consultation, including analysis of the client's hair and scalp and ensuring all testing is carried out. 2. Select the correct products and demonstrate massage techniques suitable for the client's hair and scalp type with complete autonomy. 3. Select and perform styling and finishing techniques to client's requirements. 4. Recommend products and services to client. 5. Identify, maintain and monitor good working practices, health and safety within the salon. 6. Self and peer evaluation of practical skills to enable progression, achievement and praise. **Most learners will be able to:** 1. Recognise correct cutting techniques to achieve client requirements. 2. Demonstrate the establishing and following of cutting guidelines to achieve a balanced haircut. **Some learners will be able to:** 1. Demonstrate competence of a service to VRQ Level 2 standards.

(Continued)

Figure 5.4   (Continued)

Time	Tutor activity	Learner activity	How individual learner needs will be met	Assessment
5.50	**Set-up** Check salon environment to ensure safety, hygiene and accessibility for all learners and clients. Display aims and objectives of the session. Display client services booked in on flipchart. Display positives and improvements from last session on Prezi (or flipchart if technical problems).			
6.00	**Introduction** Welcome learners verbally. Take register and check uniforms/ID. Deal with late arrivals as necessary. Introduce aims and objectives and positives and improvements from last session, and engage learners in, and facilitate discussion on how we intend to achieve them. Delegate salon manager.	Active listening and responding; Q&A if necessary. Learners take part in a whole-group discussion on how to work towards summative practical assessments (**FE),** sharing ideas and progress to date. By working as a team (**TM)** learners then help each other to work towards an agreed outcome, possibly seeking out new challenges and showing flexibility (**SM).**	Differentiated questioning to engage learners and encourage participation. Verbal and visual display of aims and objectives.	Q&A Feedback Observe social and personal skills Participation levels Level and range of verbal responses
6.10	**Main** Facilitate assignment of models to learners and preparation of salon for clients with reference to session appointments booked, previous commercial salon progress sheets and tracking data.	Setting personal targets for the session. Set up sections adhering to/using good working practices/health and safety and COSHH regulations. Prepare area for planned assessments. Completing practical task sheet/consultation sheet, making them accessible for assessor.	Guide learners using appropriate verbal/body language when necessary.	Observation Participation levels Task sheet completion
6.15	Clients to arrive at appointed times. Observe learners greeting and assessing clients' needs. Observe consultations. Distribute extension activities.	Follow all health and safety regulations. Greet and begin assessing clients' needs using consultation. Offer techniques for a commercial outcome to clients. Relay consultation outcomes to tutor to enable feedback and verbal evidence of summative/formative assessment. Active listening and responding; Q&A if necessary. Commence with services to clients, follow manufacturers' instructions and complete service to the satisfaction of the client. Ensure a safe working environment is maintained for peers.		

Figure 5.4 (Continued)

	Facilitate learning and confidence building with learners. Reinforce previous knowledge and skills. Give constructive feedback to aid progression and achievement.	Learners not working on clients to assist with formative assessment, develop skills further through extension/challenge activities of formative assessment on blocks. On completion of practical performance, tidy workstations and resources away. Complete practical session worksheet and consultation sheet. Receive feedback from assessor and file formative/summative assessment evidence.	Visual prompts/ diagrams displayed on learners' mirrors. Learners to describe using diagrams/ pictures (kinaesthetic). Auditory instructions. Probing/Socratic questioning. Questioning using Bloom's taxonomy. Modelling professionalism. Giving feedback. Encouraging problem-solving. Individual target setting. Stretch and challenge: • work towards a commercially viable timeframe • finish clients' hair using a different technique.	Formative/ Summative Observation Product of work Observe social and personal skills Participation levels Responses to Q&A Self-assessment
	Begin assessing by constantly observing and questioning techniques to build learning through Bloom's taxonomy. Aid and assist those working formatively. Observe summative performance for assessment.			
	Analyse learner performance. Provide constructive feedback to learners on their performance, focusing on achievement and areas for development to enable progression. Maintain accurate records of assessment in log books. Check learners have filled out consultation sheets. Set targets with learners for formative and summative assessments.			
8.40	Monitor salon manager's delegation of end-of-session jobs. Facilitate learners cleaning work areas after practical activity. Ensure learners effectively sterilise, sanitise and clean all tools and equipment, work surfaces and work areas.	Clean, sanitise and sterilise all work areas following all health and safety regulations Ensure a safe working environment is maintained for peers.	Guide learners using appropriate verbal/body language when necessary.	Observe social and personal skills Participation levels

(Continued)

Figure 5.4 (Continued)

8.50	Recap Facilitate recap of session using learners' evaluation of the personal targets and extension activities that were set for the session.	Taking part in whole-group and individual discussion. Listening, reading, speaking.		Observe social and personal skills Participation levels Observation Q&A
8.55	Facilitate discussion on how we achieved. Review aims and objectives. Identify positives and improvements from session. Sticky note feedback activity.	Active listening and responding. Writing responses to one thing they have enjoyed and 'what can I do for you?'	Visual, kinaesthetic, auditory.	Observe social and personal skills Participation levels Feedback (individual) Q&A

Self Evaluation of Session	
What went well?	**What could be improved?**
1. Did the learners achieve the aims/objectives (did learning take place)? 2. Did all the learners participate? 3. Did the learners enjoy the session?	1. 2. 3.
Actions to carry forward:	

A training 'SESSION' plan

1. Set-up
• Ensure the learning space is ready, safe and fit for purpose.
• Check resources and materials.
2. Enter/engage
• Share objectives for the learning and the headlines of what they will learn.
• Introduce yourself and have them introduce themselves to each other – and you, where numbers allow.
• Energiser with purpose – get the energy flowing and be sure that it is congruent with what you are trying to achieve.
3. Share subject content
• Keep new content to 'bite-sized' chunks.
• Use case studies, images, video and quotes to bring it alive.
• Focus the bulk of the time on the participants practising what you have trained them.
• Use real work and real people.
• Use a blend of individual and group work.

4. **S**ummarise
• Go back over the content delivered as a reminder, synthesise themes and highlight the key learning points.
• Share your reflections of how the training has gone – the highs and the challenges. Thank participants for their input and effort.
5. **I**ntegrate
• Get participants to reflect on what the learning means for them and how they will integrate their new skills and knowledge in their job roles.
• Encourage all participants to set SMART targets for the future to extend and consolidate their learning experience.
6. **O**utline **n**ext steps
• Explain what they should or could do next.
• Establish any follow-up work, e.g. action learning sets, follow-up workshop, coaching or mentoring session.

Figure 5.5   A training 'SESSION' plan

Activity

Consider the 'session' mnemonic to help you plan the stages of a typical training session.

Summary

In this chapter you learnt about:

- *key considerations for planning vocational learning;*
- *the tools of session planning;*
- *models of teaching;*
- *the role of initial assessment and learning styles or preference.*

Theory focus

Further reading

CAVTL (Commission on Adult Vocational Teaching and Learning) (2013) *It's About Work... Excellent Adult Vocational Teaching and Learning*. London: Learning and Skills Improvement Service.

Coffield, F, Moseley, D, Hall, E and Ecclestone, K (2004) *Should We Be Using Learning Styles? What Research has to Say to Practice*. London: Learning and Skills Research Centre.

Dweck, C (2012) *Mindset: How You Can Fulfil Your Potential*. London: Robinson Publishing.

Faraday, S, Overton, C and Cooper, S (2011) *Effective Teaching and Learning in Vocational Education*. London: LSN.

Lucas, B, Spencer, E and Claxton, G (2012) *How to Teach Vocational Education: A Theory of Vocational Pedagogy*. London: City and Guilds Centre for Skills Development.

Petty, G (2009) *Evidence-Based Teaching: A Practical Approach*. London: Nelson Thornes.

Websites

Functional skills criteria: www2.ofqual.gov.uk/downloads/category/68-functional-skills-subject-criteria

Health and Safety Executive: www.hse.gov.uk/risk

Mindset: www.mindsetonline.com

Centre for Skills Development: www.skillsdevelopment.org

Centre for Real-World Learning: www.winchester.ac.uk/aboutus/lifelonglearning/CentreforRealWorldLearning

A guide to learning styles: www.vark-learn.com

References

Barton, D and Hamilton, M (1998) *Local Literacies: Reading and Writing in One Community*. London: Routledge.

Beetham, H and Oliver, M (2010) 'The Changing Practices of Knowledge and Learning', in R. Sharpe and H. Beetham (Eds) *Rethinking Learning for a Digital Age*, pp. 155–169, London: RoutledgeFalmer.

Duckworth, V (2013a) *Learning Trajectories, Violence and Empowerment amongst Adult Basic Skills Learners*. Education Research Monograph. London: Routledge.

Dweck, C S (2006) *Mindset: The New Psychology of Success*. New York: Random House.

Faraday S, Overton C and Cooper S (2011) *Effective Teaching and Learning in Vocational Education*. London: LSN.

Fleming, N D (2001) *Teaching and Learning Styles: VARK Strategies*. Christchurch, New Zealand: N D Fleming.

Gee, J P (1996) *Social Linguistics and Literacies: Ideology in Discourses* (Second Edition). London: RoutledgeFalmer.

Petty, G (2006) *Evidence-based Teaching*. Cheltenham: Nelson Thornes.

Street, B (1984) *Literacy in Theory and Practice*. Cambridge: Cambridge University Press.

6 EXPERIENTIAL AND APPLIED LEARNING

In this chapter you will learn about:

- the experiential learning cycle;
- the flipped classroom;
- learning by practising, real-world problem solving, being coached, reflection, virtual environments, competing, simulation and playing games, and co-operative learning.

Professional Standards

Standard 5: Develop and prepare resources for learning and development – KU1 The different types of resources that can be used to support learning across the full range of the training cycle

Standard 7: Facilitate individual learning and development – KU10 How to support different types of learners in applying new or enhanced learning in context

Introduction

Tell me and I'll forget. Show me and I'll remember. Involve me and I'll understand.

There are different terms used to label the process of learning from experience. Education philosopher John Dewey (1915) discussed the power and impact of 'learning by doing' not just listening or watching. Pring (in Lucas *et al.*, 2012: 79) identifies how learning by doing is different from doing theory and then applying it, where correction from experienced others allows the vocational learner to meet and internalise professional standards. In this chapter, we consider both the value of experience acquired through learning by doing and applied learning.

As we explored in Chapter 1, vocational education and training is often characterised by its links to the real world of work and the development of a working competence in skills related to a particular sector or job role. Experiential learning is generally accepted as the hands-on experience you obtain by applying theoretical knowledge in a real-world setting. Applied learning activities provide learners with the opportunity to learn from an experience.

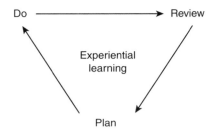

Figure 6.1   The cycle of experiential learning

> *Applied learning involves acquiring and applying knowledge, skills and understanding through tasks set in sector contexts that have many of the characteristics of real work, or are set within the workplace. Most importantly, the purpose of the task in which learners apply their knowledge, skills and understanding must be relevant to real work in the sector. (QCA, 2007)*

We would suggest that learners only learn from experiences they believe are truly relevant to them. Experiential learning facilitates this as it is the process of making meaning from direct experience. Education theorist David Kolb (1984) proposed a four-stage model or cycle of experience learning.

For Kolb, experiential learning is *the process whereby knowledge is created through the transformation of experience. Knowledge results from the combination of grasping and transforming experience* (Kolb, 1984: 41). This model is simple to apply and its common-sense learning from experience approach appeals to both new and experienced practitioners.

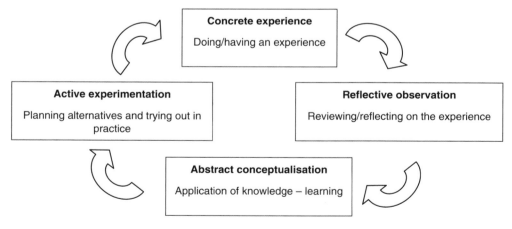

Figure 6.2   Kolb's experiential learning cycle

When planning your programme of vocational education, it is important to consider how you will provide learners with regular opportunities for practical and applied learning in order to promote learning through experience.

You might consider a range of different learning strategies, involving employers, role models, work experience, role-play, competitions, games and real-world scenarios. Real-life case studies can also provide a mechanism for learners to apply their developing vocational knowledge and understanding.

Lucas, Spencer and Claxton (2012) identify a number of learning and teaching methods that may support an experiential and applied learning approach to vocational education and training:

- learning by practising;

- learning through real-world problem-solving;

- learning by being coached;

- learning through reflection;

- learning through virtual environments;

- learning by competing;

- learning through simulation and playing games.

Learning through practice and real-world problem-solving

Many vocational education providers provide a range of realistic working environments to give learners lots of opportunities to get hands on and learn through experience and practice. Hospitality and catering learners often benefit from a professional kitchen and working restaurant open to real clients for lunches, dinners and special events. Motor vehicle learners often learn, through their experience in the workshop, to apply their knowledge and skills on real vehicles, perhaps working with real clients to take orders, complete jobs and evaluate their performance.

Learners following study programmes in hairdressing and beauty therapy can often practise their practical skills in professional salons, meeting the needs of real clients who want professional services. Tutors provide an essential role as facilitators, ensuring that learners' practice is safe and appropriate.

Learners studying on travel and tourism courses benefit from opportunities to practise their skills in mock aircraft cabins or on coach trips and visits, relaying safety information to clients, carrying out safety demonstrations and using industry-standard equipment.

The creation of authentic tasks and activities, utilising real clients where possible, gives learners the opportunity to solve problems and dilemmas they are likely to find in the real world. This helps to develop a working competence that will be useful in preparing them for future employment and higher-level study. Tutors can develop a problem-based learning (PBL) approach to stretch and challenge the vocational skills of learners as they become more competent in dealing with the routine and expected.

What opportunities do your learners have to practise their developing vocational skills? Do you have the equipment and resources to make the learning experience professional and in line with industry expectations? If not, can you identify links and partnerships with other providers that may provide opportunities for application and practice?

Learning through virtual learning environments (VLE)

The use of VLEs has developed quickly across the FE and Skills sector. Where the higher education sector predominately utilises commercial products for their virtual environments, such as Blackboard (www.blackboard.com), the majority of the FE sector has been drawn towards an open source solution called Moodle (www.moodle.org).

Whichever system is used, most VLEs (or course/learner management systems as they are sometimes known) provide a range of sophisticated teaching, learning and assessment options. Multimedia content can be uploaded to provide a range of independent and guided learning options which can be accessed from anywhere in the world with an internet connection and a computer device. The use of online material, video and audio can be integrated to provide an interactive learning experience.

These learning options can take advantage of both synchronous (real time) and asynchronous (non-real time) learning. A range of tools can be used to interact and communicate with learners on a one-to-one basis or with a whole group, cohort, department or year group.

Table 6.1 Tools for interacting with learners online

	Synchronous (real time)	**Asynchronous (non-real time)**
One-to-many	Chat room Online whiteboard	Announcements Messages Emails Discussion boards Forums Blogs
One-to-one	Instant messages Chat Online whiteboard	Personal messages Emails

More and more vocational education providers are looking towards their VLEs to make cost savings, provide flexible learning experiences and motivate learners. As the environments are virtual, there are opportunities for learners to develop and practise their vocational skills in a safe, risk-free environment. The interactive features of VLEs also support the popular notion of the 'flipped classroom' experience.

The flipped classroom

The increased use of the internet, VLEs, online resources and multimedia for learning has facilitated a shift in how precious face-to-face learning time is best used. Whether this be in the classroom, workshop, salon or pitch, time with learners to build relationships, to facilitate the application of skills and to answer questions is critical to effective learning experiences. To maximise the use of this time at a time of funding restrictions and increased time pressures, many practitioners are considering some of the concepts of the 'flipped classroom' model.

Taking a 'flipped' approach to teaching and learning, rather than spending the session time delivering a lecture to a whole group of learners, this knowledge transmission role is replaced by a video, featuring presentation visuals (such as slides) and audio narration. Learners engage with the multimedia resources in their own time through their computers or mobile devices and then spend the time in the face-to-face session engaged in more collaborative and interactive activities. The tutor becomes the facilitator of learning, the 'guide on the side', rather than the transmitter of knowledge, or the 'sage on the stage'.

Activity

Explore the EDUCAUSE guide to '7 things you should know about the flipped classroom' and then consider one of your own units that you currently teach. Could you develop multimedia resources to support a more 'flipped' approach to your curriculum design? What are the advantages and disadvantages for your learners?

Visit: www.educause.edu/library/resources/7-things-you-should-know-about-flipped-classrooms

Case study

Sandra is a lecturer in Information Technology at a large general FE college.

The IT sector changes rapidly and it is necessary to ensure that the key learning outcomes of each unit or module reflect this. In Information Technology, I have found that learners are aware of the use of personal social networking (using sites like Facebook for example) and the power of mobile and smart phone

(Continued)

(Continued)

technologies but not online applications. I have encouraged learners to use 'cloud applications' to improve collaborative learning. Cloud applications are stored on central servers and accessed through any internet-enabled device. They allow multiple users to work on the same document, project or template. The fact that two or more people can work on the same IT project at the same time replicates the work environment as large ICT projects are developed by teams. An example is Prezi.com. The topic of equality and diversity is an important issue within FE and I used Prezi as a tool for Level 3 learners to work together, under a team leader, to develop and deliver a presentation on equality and diversity in the workplace.

This showed them how ICT training sessions could be developed and delivered for a variety of topics. They were also able to see how they could develop ideas by working together at the same time so that the project grows in front of them during the development stage rather than reviewing and amending each stage once the project has been completed.

ICT involves learning both theory and the practical components. How to reinforce the theory in a practical way can be an issue. Many of my learners like working practically. They want to be on the computers, making websites, creating code and designing graphics. Spending time ensuring they understand the theoretical

Figure 6.3   Equality and diversity presentation using Prezi

components can be difficult. One effective way of managing the IT room environment is through the use of specialist software which allows me to control the computer screens of each learner. I am able to use the software to broadcast my presentation on screen to theirs. This removes the temptation to be looking at Facebook or checking emails during my delivery!

I also find the use of interactive teaching tools very useful in engaging my learners. Tools such as Triptico (www.triptico.co.uk) allow me to set engaging challenges that recap key points from previous lessons or to introduce the learning objectives for the current lesson. The use of the interactive tools has made a big difference to my lessons' success. Lateness and lack of focus at the beginning of a lesson has been a problem. Now by having a 10–20 minute interactive session, e.g. using the Triptico Spinning Wheel application, to stimulate discussion or act as a quiz, means that learners want to arrive before the start of the lesson to make sure they can take part and are learning by being actively engaged in the process.

Learners can come to the whiteboard and develop their own activity using Triptico tools and the ability to control their own learning has empowered them. The rate of learning has increased, my stress levels have decreased! The learners are working harder and I am becoming more of a facilitator.

Activity

Check out the free interactive tutor resources available from the Triptico site – www.triptico.co.uk. Explore the tools and consider how they could be used in your session, either as a starter, in the main body or as a revision or recap tool.

Consider your vocational qualification specification. Do you have aspects of your syllabus that learners find less engaging, less practical or dull? What approaches might you use to engage and motivate your learners through experiential learning activities?

Learning by being coached

An experienced and knowledgeable coach can be an invaluable resource for vocational learners developing the standards of their applied and practical skills. In many vocational subjects, you will act as the coach, modelling, correcting, guiding and advising on the best techniques, the habits to avoid, how to use the materials and tools of your trade. As coach, you are also likely to provide emotional support and encouragement when things go wrong, mistakes happen and motivation levels take a nose-dive.

You can also encourage learners to coach each other, to pose questions, to negotiate targets and to identify actions. Whitmore (2003) is credited with developing the popular 'GROW' coaching model which aims to unlock potential following a cycle that explores an individuals' Goals, Reality, Opportunities and Will to commit.

Table 6.2   Whitmore's GROW model

Goal	What do you want to achieve?
	What would achieving this lead to in the long term?
	When would you like to achieve this by?
Reality	What is your current position?
	What stops you from moving on?
Options	What could you do?
	What else?
	And what else?
Will	What will you do?
	What will be the first step?

Tolhurst (2010) proposes the LEAP model as a useful alternative framework:

L – Looking at goals

E – Exploring reality

A – Analysing possibilities

P – Planning action

Coaching then, can be an ongoing process of correction and guidance and learners engage in practical activity to develop their skills. It can also be a part of a formalised process, using models and frameworks to guide learners to identify targets, change their practice and overcome barriers to achieve them. For many, the coaching process is a way of learning about oneself, how we learn and how we can improve our own learning strategies. These meta-learning skills will equip learners with the resilience and confidence to succeed in their chosen vocations.

Case study

Helen is a freelance vocational trainer in management and leadership.

I have worked for more than 20 years in the FMCG (fast moving consumer goods) industry for a variety of large companies which manufacture famous brands in sectors such as soft drinks and crisps and snacks. After starting my career in sales, I then moved into marketing and became a senior leader in a large private limited company. I am now working as an organisational consultant and executive coach.

Throughout my career I have supported others on their learning journeys through formal training and coaching as part of my line manager role. Industry training tended to be vocational and focused on the participants learning new skills to apply in their roles to improve performance.

I now train and coach other consultants in skills specific to their roles. In my experience, vocational training should focus on learning not the training. The spotlight of my attention should be on the participants and on their learning, not on what I am doing and what comes next. This takes practice and is not always easy but the participants notice the difference, they learn more and feedback will usually be better as a result.

I was once told that people rarely remember more than one or two significant things from a training session and reflecting on my own experience I concluded there is something in that statement. This has influenced the way I design a session. My intention is always to keep the 'tell' or 'push' content to a small number of big ideas then use them as a skeleton around which to build the learning experience. I then ask the learner to make their contribution when applying their learning. There should be a clear motivator for the learner to be engaging in the training, this way they can 'pull' the content they need, by asking questions and trying to solve problems which are relevant to their own roles and contexts.

I recently attended a workshop where an eminent psychologist talked about neuroscience and the nature of change. This is not an easy subject to convey as you might imagine – even to a room full of coaches who work with clients on their change journeys every day.

I learnt from this session the importance of keeping training sessions simple. He used everyday colloquial language that we could understand easily. He shared

(Continued)

(Continued)

lots of stories which were really engaging and often very funny to make his points, and he kept the number of PowerPoint slides to a minimum. Often training confuses more than it enlightens, so I take significant time to think about how I can keep my session simple for learners.

When a trainer takes a transition mode to delivery, they are often focused on sending their energy out towards the whole room in general. They are not differentiating one learner from another. This is not a very personal experience for the learner and the experience can feel very superficial. When energy is flowing both ways, the trainer and participants are truly connecting. The trainer will feel that they are 'in flow' or 'in the zone' and the participants will be truly engaged.

Some ideas I use for ensuring that the energy flows both ways:

- *Posture and breathing – stand in a way in which you feel grounded and comfortable and breathe easily, ideally from your diaphragm/lower belly rather than your chest.*

- *Have a 'conversation' with the participants – rather than 'train' them.*

- *Be curious about their responses – give them airtime and deeply listen to them.*

- *'Invite them into the room' – ask them to share their own experiences and knowledge of the subject they are learning about. This is really powerful.*

I often use a technique called 'appreciative inquiry'. I ask them what they like about the subject and what is going well for them. When debriefing exercises I tend to get all the participants involved and ask them what they liked about each other's work. This approach helps to focus on the positives in a situation and what works, rather than getting bogged down in problems, issues and barriers. By sharing success stories and solutions, the whole group can share good practice, collect new ways of working and further develop existing effective practice.

I find case studies are a wonderful way to enable participants to practise their learning. Where possible I use case studies, which are based on real situations – even though sometimes I have to anonymise them to protect confidentiality. When learners know it is real it somehow seems to engage them some more.

As well as real case studies, the use of real people in learning can be a powerful tool. When training in selling skills for example, the use of real customers can be a great way for learners to practise their new skills in as real a situation as possible, while ensuring maximum safety. When training research skills, I ask learners to lead a real focus group and collect real data.

I consistently hear that this is the real magic dust in a learning experience – and it is very rare too.

I try to ensure my design for learning is congruent with what I want to achieve and the subject being learned. For example, on a training session with executives on how to be more creative and innovative, I ensure my approach is innovative and the learning environment is in a creative space wherever possible. When I train people in coaching skills, I ensure there are opportunities for learners to apply their skills by coaching each other.

So that the training experience is most effective, I always ask my course participants to reflect on what they have learned at the end of the training and share it with other participants. I often ask them to think about what they have learned, what surprised them and what they will do differently.

Then to follow up, I ensure they have coaching support – perhaps from a line manager or subject matter expert. The use of 'action learning sets' can really help them to embed their learning.

Learning through reflection

As highlighted in Kolb's (1984) experiential cycle, taking time to reflect on a concrete experience is an important learning process in making meaning and developing a deeper understanding. Building on the work of Dewey (1933), Schön (1983) highlights two useful forms of reflective practice: 'reflection-in-action' and 'reflection-on-action'. Reflection-in-action *involves thinking about action while actually executing it, which may result in modification to the action while it is in progress* (Schön, 1983: 50). For the vocational learner, reflection-in-action could be taken during a practical workshop session, to modify practice or process to improve the outcome. For example, in a busy training kitchen, the catering learner will continually reflect on their experiential learning, adding ingredients to taste, responding to orders filtering through from the restaurant, reacting to others in the busy catering team and what's going on around them.

Post-event reflections could be seen as 'reflection-on-action'. Reflection-on-action *involves thinking back and talking about the actions, which may result in subsequent actions of a similar type being modified in the light of such reflection* (Schön 1983: p.50). For the vocational learner, this could be the post-practical session evaluation process, where a critical reflection of the session is carried out in terms of the effectiveness of skills application. For example, the trainee hairdresser will reflect on the busy salon session, the level of client satisfaction, the accuracy of the cuts, how well they worked as part of a team and the professionalism of service given. By reflecting on their experience, changes, tweaks and improvements can be identified, planned and implemented next time, developing skills further in an attempt to develop working competence.

Gibbs (1988) offers a model for reflection or a 'reflection cycle' based on the work of Kolb. Gibb's six-stage model provides a useful framework when reflecting on 'concrete experiences' such as practical sessions, for example:

1. Description – what happened.

2. Feelings – what were you thinking and feeling.

3. Evaluation – what was good and bad about the experience.

4. Analysis – what sense can you make of the situation.

5. Conclusion – what else could you have done.

6. Action plan – if it arose again, what would you do.

Brookfield (1995) offers a model of reflection based on the consideration of different perspectives of an experience. The 'critical lenses for reflection' model identifies four different points of view, or critical lenses, which should be taken into consideration when reflecting on an experience. For the vocational learner, reflecting using this model could involve considering the outcomes of the learning experience from a range of perspectives:

- Autobiography – what are the learners' own thoughts and opinions of the experience?

- Tutors'/employers' eyes – what is the feedback from the experienced, dual professionals?

- Peer perceptions – what do our colleagues think and feel about our skills and performance?

- Theoretical, philosophical and research literature – what does the theory suggest?

Adding to the debate on the importance of reflective practice, we propose our own framework to guide and shape reflection on practice that may lead to positive development and impact. The Independent Reflective Investigation for Solution(s) model (IRIS) encourages learners to take a solutions-based approach to addressing barriers or concerns to their developing vocational practice. Four sequential lenses are presented to guide reflectors to consider how their existing strengths and on-going skills development can be used to identify an intervention. The model encourages learners to move through the flow of reflection, focusing on how interventions may be implemented practically and what impact they may have on future practice.

Stage 1: Incident
Learners should identify a particular critical incident from their practice or experience to reflect on. They should describe the incident—what are their concerns? Have they identified a barrier to success?

Stage 2: Intervention
Having identified an incidence of their practice, learners should consider an intervention that might address the concerns. How can this intervention build on their existing strengths? What skills might they need to develop and who could support them to move through the flow? For example, tutor, mentor, coach, employer.

Stage 3: Implement
Having identified a possible intervention, how might the learner practically implement this in their vocational practice? What could tutors and employers do to make it happen? What practical and logistical consideration do they need to address?

Stage 4: Impact
Finally, learners should consider what impact the intervention might have on their future practice. What would success look like? Are there any areas of risk? How will they measure the impact? Was the implementation successful? Do they have any further concerns?

Depending on the outcome, reflectors can return to each stage of the model to refine and develop their reflections and their practice.

Use the IRIS model of reflection template (Appendix 3) and go through each stage as a learner yourself. What aspect of your own practice or experience might you want to reflect on and scrutinise. Consider possible interventions, how these might be implemented and what the impact would look like on your day-to-day role. You might consider an approach to teaching and training vocational learners as your critical incident.

Learning through competing

The World Skills Foundation organises and co-ordinates the International World Skills challenge every two years. Hundreds of vocational learners from across the world, accompanied by their tutors, come together to compete before the public in the skills of their various trades, testing themselves against challenging international standards. They represent the best of their peers drawn from regional and national skill competitions in over 65 different countries.

World Skills UK – The Skills Show provides a challenging showcase of vocational excellence from learners across the country. The winner of this competition decides the UK team who will compete in the International World Skills challenge.

> Alongside other activities such as enterprise education, work experience and cultural experiences, skills competitions can contribute to setting clear and stretching targets for learning and achievement. It has also proven to contribute towards 'outstanding' Ofsted inspections. Competitions activity increases the employability of learners, provides access to international teaching and learning resources and raises the profile of Apprenticeships and vocational learning. (World Skills UK, 2013)

Table 6.3   The 46 competitive vocational skills areas at World Skills UK

Construction and building technology	Plastering and drywall systems
	Refrigeration and air-conditioning
	Landscape gardening
	Carpentry
	Joinery
	Cabinet making
	Painting and decorating
	Architectural stonemasonry
	Bricklaying
	Electrical installations
	Plumbing and heating
	Wall and floor tiling

(Continued)

Table 6.3   (Continued)

Creative arts and fashion	Visual merchandising/window dressing
	Graphic design technology
	Fashion technology
	Floristry
	Jewellery
Information and communication technology	Print media technology
	Information network cabling
	IT network systems administration
	Web design
	IT software solutions for business
Manufacturing and engineering technology	Plastic die engineering
	Prototype modelling
	Sheet metal technology
	Construction metal work
	Mobile robotics
	Electronics
	Welding
	CNC milling
	CNC turning
	Mechanical engineering design – CAD
	Mechatronics
	Manufacturing team challenge
	Polymechanics/automation
	Industrial control
Social and personal services	Health and social care
	Restaurant service
	Cooking
	Confectioner/pastry cook
	Beauty therapy
	Hairdressing
Transportation and logistics	Aircraft maintenance
	Car painting
	Automobile technology
	Autobody repair

Activity

Explore the World Skills UK website and identify the steps required to enter your own learners in a national skills competition.

Consider the value of arranging an internal skills competition in your own college, prison or private training provider. What would be the advantages and what resources would you need to make it happen?

Visit: http://World Skills uk.apprenticeships.org.uk

As well as World Skills, other events help to raise the profile of vocational learning, celebrate achievement and highlight the development and showcasing of professional skills.

VQ Day (www.vqday.org.uk)

Launched in 2008 to raise the status of practical and vocational learning and to celebrate vocational achievement, VQ Day is a national celebration of vocational qualifications for learners, tutors and employers. Organised by the technical, practical and vocational learning charity Edge Foundation, VQ Day helps to recognise the millions of talented and skilled people throughout the UK who are awarded vocational qualifications (VQs) each year.

Activity

Explore the VQ website and focus on the VQ award winners. Highlight those who could be useful vocational role models for your own learners.

Adult Learners' Week (www.alw.org.uk)

Organised by NIACE, Adult Learners' Week is a national celebration of the benefits of FE and Skills. Thousands of events are run during the week each year to recognise the achievement of outstanding adult learners and to raise the profile of different kinds of adult learning, including: progress at work; keeping fit; improving health; supporting a family; helping the community; being creative and developing self and others.

Each year, award winners are selected from many inspirational stories of dedication and achievement in adult education and training, including adult apprentices.

National Apprenticeship week (www.apprenticeships.org.uk)

Co-ordinated by the National Apprenticeship Service (NAS), National Apprenticeship Week is designed to celebrate apprenticeships and the positive impact they have on individuals and businesses. Employers are encouraged to get involved in a variety of ways to promote the benefits of apprenticeships and vocational learning. Employer-led events include:

- job swaps and 'back to the floor' events;

- apprenticeship halls of fame;

- open days and job shadowing events;

- employer challenges.

Learning through playing games

As well as learning through competitions, games and simulations can provide valuable opportunities for learners to practise and develop their skills in a 'safe' environment where making mistakes is expected and does not lead to difficult and costly problems! Games can be traditional, making use of human and physical resources to solve problems and dilemmas. More commonly today, games frequently involve computers, software and other technologies to provide interactive and engaging learning opportunities which harness the power of play. These so-called 'serious games' are the focus of much on-going research.

Work by FutureLab (2013) into the role of computer games for learning suggests that game-based learning can improve engagement and motivation but does not necessarily improve attainment. They identify a number of recommendations for integrating gaming into teaching, supported by a clear pedagogic process. In particular:

- Place learning activities and academic content within the video game's fictional and entertainment context, maintaining a balance between fun and learning.

- Make the academic content integral to the game rather than an add-on. Content-specific tasks work better when embedded in the fictional context and rules ('mechanics') of the game.

- Carefully plan the roles that you and your learners will take on in the game. Tutors should play roles that allow them to mediate the experience for learners: providing guidance when needed; ensuring that rules are followed; and maintaining a respectful atmosphere.

- Don't try to divorce decontextualised components of a game (such as badges, scores, leader boards) from the fictional context and rules of the game (the 'mechanics').

The 'game' of the flight simulator is a commonly understood example where pilots in training use sophisticated computer software and equipment to develop their skills in flying and landing aircraft. Simulation games are commonly used for medical professionals when first practising certain procedures and processes which trainees would be unable to carry out on real patients initially. The use of advanced technologies, such as augmented and virtual realities, provides new and exciting opportunities for realistic simulated experiences to develop practical skills. The virtual world of Second Life (www.secondlife.com) provides a virtual environment where millions of people across the world participate in realistic games, simulations and experiences.

Case study

Lenny is a freelance vocational trainer who believes in the power of play for learning.

As an educator and trainer, I am fascinated by play. I'm fascinated by the games we play; by the similarity and differences in games across time and culture; and by who we chose to play with and who we will not play with. But what fascinates me the most is how we learn through play, and how play creates community.

Play in education is often seen as the realm of Early Years. As children we learn so much through play or at least a playful exploration of the world. We learn to count by playing 'shops' and we practise our social skills in games like mums and dads, schools and goodies v. baddies. Biologists and behavioural psychologists have known for some time that our brains are hardwired to learn through play; that when we play we develop both socially and emotionally as well as cognitively. Our education policy and practice in Early Years reflects this.

It is clear however, that as learners get older, we use play as an educational tool less and less. I feel this is one of the biggest mistakes that we make as practitioners. Serious games are games that are designed to develop a solution or an intervention to a real-world problem. One example of a serious game is a programme called Foldit, which has been developed by the University of Washington. Foldit is an online video game where participants get to play with, or fold, the structures of protein molecules in order to create a three-dimensional model of what that protein looks like.

Foldit allows amateur scientists the opportunity to develop three-dimensional models of proteins. And why is this important? Scientists have spent the best part of a decade trying to figure out the structure of a particular protein that causes HIV. Knowing the structure of this protein would have implications for developing effective antiviral drugs. This problem was put into the gaming programme Foldit and within ten days three players, three amateur scientists, had come up with a viable model for the structure of this protein.

What Foldit demonstrates is that a well-designed game, whether played in the digital world or the real world, can literally make us smarter. A well-designed game can lead us to approach a problem more creatively or critically than we otherwise would have. A well-designed game allows us to successfully collaborate with others, building on the success and failures of others. Crucially, a well-designed game enables us to learn from our failures, seeing our failures as prototypes – these are all critical skills that learners need to develop regardless of the subject being studied.

I have played games with a range of learners of different abilities from secondary school pupils right up to undergraduates. Playing games with learners enables them to engage in a way that does not happen without games. Learners become immersed, excited. They have a real desire to see the next bit of the puzzle or scenario unfold. Most importantly, the game gives learners an emotional, kinaesthetic and tangible experience from which to develop their learning.

(Continued)

(Continued)

The other great thing about play is that it creates community. We are social animals with a strong desire to make connections with others. Play gives us the perfect opportunity to do this. In order to realise how powerful play can be to create community, we need only remember what it felt like when we were told by a group of friends that were playing together, that we could not join in.

We also know how games can create community through sporting events; as a player or supporter in a school, local or national team; or even as a spectator of a major event such as the Olympics. Games give people a sense of belonging and a desire to be part of something bigger. This not only happens in sport but also when a group of friends go paintballing together, or when hundreds of people participate in community events.

Playing games with learners enables them to build trust and respect for each other, which in turn further supports their learning. This is the very premise of 'team building'. When we play together, we learn something about ourselves and the other people playing the game that enables us to relate to each other differently. Most tutors will 'do' team-building activities in 'induction week' and expect that to be enough to last a cohort through a one-, even two-year course. You wouldn't build a house and not expect to maintain it. In the same way why would you build a team and not expect to maintain it. Things will go wrong within your group of learners. There will be fallouts, groups and cliques will form and some learners will have very little interaction with other learners both inside and outside the classroom. Whilst much of this will be outside your control, by regularly playing games, you will enable your learners to strengthen and rebuild relationships.

Games need to be well designed in order to produce the best results. Games work best that are collaborative in nature rather than games that can be polarising. This is not to say that games cannot be competitive. Competition can help individuals and groups strive to improve. However, if at any stage in a game or activity, learners feel that they cannot 'win', whatever winning looks like, then they will become demotivated and disengaged.

What does this mean then for our education policies and practice? Pat Kane, author of The Play Ethic (2004) states that play will be to the 21st century what work was to the industrial age – our dominant way of knowing, doing and creating value. Our education policies and practice need to prepare our learners not simply for the world in which we live today, but the emerging new world. The world that we don't yet know.

Our need is to be adaptive, confident problem solvers. Games can and do create such learners but for both the tutor and the learner to have confidence in learning through play, we need to create new narratives of play. We must not allow play to be seen as the domain of the Early Years sector and we must respect play as a legitimate tool for learning, regardless of age. Games must become a part of the tutor's and learner's toolkit.

Think about your own vocational subject and your current practice. Do you harness the power of play in your approach to teaching and learning?

Could you introduce a 'serious game' to your approach to develop learners' skills and sense of community?

Would your game be traditional or make use of learning technologies, the internet and virtual worlds?

Co-operative teaching and learning

Co-operative learning may be broadly defined as any classroom learning situation in which learners of all levels of performance work together in structured groups toward a shared or common goal. In classrooms where collaboration is practised, learners pursue learning in groups of varying size: negotiating, initiating, planning and evaluating together. Rather than working as individuals in competition with every other individual in the classroom, learners are given the responsibility of creating a learning community where all learners participate in important and meaningful ways.

Co-operative learning requires that learners work together to achieve goals that they could not achieve individually. It is a way for learners to learn essential interpersonal life skills and to develop the ability to work collaboratively, a skill which is in demand in the workplace. It is a way for learners to take turns with different roles such as facilitator, scribe, reporter, etc. In a co-operative group, every learner has a specific task; everyone must be involved in the learning or project.

Strategies to promote effective co-operative learning and teaching include:

- Establish rapport.

The first step that you need to take is to establish a positive relationship with your class. Get to know their hobbies, what job they want to progress to, any barriers they may have etc.

- Establish clear group objectives.

Effective collaborative learning involves establishment of group goals, as well as individual responsibility. This ensures that they keep on task and establishes an explicit purpose. Before beginning the task it ensures that the objectives are clearly defined.

- Develop trust and promote open communication.

Successful interpersonal communication should be promoted in the class and groups. To do this building trust is vital. Deal with emotional issues that happen immediately and any interpersonal difficulties before moving on. Projects should encourage team members to explain concepts thoroughly to each other in a clear and meaningful way. Open communication is absolutely vital in co-operative approaches.

How can you plan for co-operative approaches?

Learners typically work in teams, which are usually composed of between four and six members. This way, they can break into pairs for some activities, and then get back together in teams very quickly for others. It is important, however, to establish classroom norms and protocols that guide learners to:

- contribute;
- stay on task;
- help each other;
- encourage each other;
- share;
- solve problems;
- give and accept feedback from peers.

A way to start co-operative learning is to begin with pairs instead of whole teams. Two learners can learn to work effectively on activities such as the following:

1. Assign a subject-specific worksheet with problems they need to address and ask learners to work in pairs.

2. One of the learners does the first problem while the second acts as a coach.

3. Then learners switch roles for the second problem.

4. When they finish the second problem, they get together with another pair and check answers.

5. When both pairs have agreed on the answers, ask them to shake hands and continue working in pairs on the next two problems.

Other strategies include the 'jigsaw' approach:

1. Select a topic, concept, theme, issue and break it into parts (e.g. unemployment – short-term causes, long-term causes, short-term effects, long-term effects).

2. Place learners in 'expert groups'.

3. Assign each group a piece of the 'puzzle' (e.g. short-term causes, long-term causes...) and ask them to develop an expertise in that piece.

4. Send individual 'experts' into mixed groups (ones with different expertise) and have them discuss and share their expertise.

Activity

Consider the teaching strategies that you use to develop active and co-operative learning in your sessions. Consider the process of peer observation where you expand your range of strategies through working with other tutors, both experienced and new. What other forms of professional development could you use to expand your vocational tutor toolkit?

Summary

In this chapter you have learnt about:

- *the experiential learning cycle;*

- *the flipped classroom;*

- *learning by practising, real-world problem-solving, being coached, reflection, virtual environments, competing, simulation and playing games, and co-operative learning.*

Theory focus

Further reading

Dweck, C (2012) *Mindset: How You Can Fulfil Your Potential*. London: Robinson Publishing.

Eastwood, L, Coates, J, Dixon, L and Harvey, J (2009) *A Toolkit for Creative Teaching in Post-Compulsory Education*. London: Open University Press.

Kane, P (2004) *The Play Ethic: A Manifesto For a Different Way of Living*. London: MacMillan.

Kehoe, D (2007) *Practice Makes Perfect: The Importance of Practical Learning*. London: The Social Market Foundation.

Perrotta, C, Featherstone, G, Aston, H and Houghton, E (2013). *Game-based Learning:*

Latest Evidence and Future Directions. Slough: NFER.

Roffey-Barentsen, J and Malthouse, R (2013) *Reflective Practice in Education and Training*. Exeter: Learning Matters.

Tolhurst, J (2010) *The Essential Guide to Coaching and Mentoring* (Second Edition). London: Pearson Education Limited.

Tummons, J and Duckworth, V (2012) *Doing your Research Project in the Lifelong Learning Sector*. Maidenhead: Open University Press.

Websites

Fold IT: www.fold.it

FutureLab: www.futurelab.org.uk

WorldSkills: www.worldskills.org

Adult Learners' Week: www.alw.org.uk

References

Brookfield, S (1995) *Becoming a Critically Reflective Teacher*. San Francisco: Jossey-Bass.

Dewey, J (1915) *Schools of Tomorrow*. New York: E P Dutton & Co.

Dewey, J (1933) *How We Think. A Restatement of the Relation of Reflective Thinking to the Educative Process* (Revised Edition). Boston: D C Heath.

Gibbs, G (1988) *Learning by Doing: A Guide to Teaching and Learning Methods*. Oxford: Further Education Unit, Oxford Polytechnic.

Kane, P (2004) *The Play Ethic: A Manifesto For a Different Way of Living*. London: MacMillan.

Kolb, D (1984) *Experiential Learning: Experience as the Source of Learning and Development*. Englewood Cliffs, NJ: Prentice Hall.

Lucas, B, Spencer, E and Claxton, G (2012) *How to Teach Vocational Education: A Theory of Vocational Pedagogy*. London: City and Guilds Centre for Skills Development.

Perrotta, C, Featherstone, G, Aston, H and Houghton, E (2013) *Game-based Learning: Latest Evidence and Future Directions* (NFER Research Programme: Innovation in Education). Slough: NFER.

QCA (2007) *The Specialised Diploma*. London: Qualifications and Curriculum Authority.

Schön, D A (1983) *The Reflective Practitioner: How Professionals Think in Action*. New York: Basic Books.

Tolhurst, J (2010) *The Essential Guide to Coaching and Mentoring* (Second Edition). London: Pearson Education Limited.

Whitmore, J. (2003) *Coaching for Performance*. London: Nicholas Brealey Publishing.

World Skills (2013) *I Am Rewarding Real Talent: An introduction for Schools, Colleges and Training Providers*. London: The National Apprenticeship Service.

7 VOCATIONAL ASSESSMENT

In this chapter you will learn about:

- why, what and how to assess vocational learners;
- modular, linear and synoptic assessment;
- initial, formative and summative assessment;
- writing vocational assignment briefs;
- giving feedback.

Professional Standards

Standard 5: Develop and prepare resources for learning and development – KU10

The contribution and challenges that technology can make to the development and adaptation of different types of resources and the challenges posed by these

Standard 8: Engage and support learners in the learning and development process – KU14 Different methods of providing the learner with constructive feedback and how to use these methods effectively

Standard 9: Assess learner achievement – KU10 How to make sure that assessment decisions are made against specified criteria and are valid, reliable and fair

Standard 11: Internally monitor and maintain the quality of assessment – KU11 The types of feedback, support and advice that assessors need and how to meet these needs

Standard 12 Externally monitor and maintain the quality of assessment – KU1 The key concepts and principles of assessment

Introduction

In general education, the final (or summative) assessment is very often a traditional written exam. In vocational education and training, there are many more opportunities for both summative and on-going (formative) assessments of knowledge, understanding and skills. When considering approaches to assessment, it is critical to understand how people learn, what they have in fact learned, and whether this knowledge is useful for their particular chosen path.

Policy around assessment methods for accredited courses has undergone recent changes, with a move away from modularised assessment to linear assessments taken at the end of programmes. For many learners following GCSE and A-level programmes, summative assessment may all take place at the end of two years of study.

Table 7.1   Assessment approaches

Assessment approach	What is it?
Modular	Where a qualification is achieved through the attainment of individual modules or units assessment, taken at different points throughout the length of the study programme. Individual module assessments are often re-taken if the first result is not desirable. Modular assessment is often criticised for fragmenting subjects and topics and reducing the opportunity for joined-up thinking and seeing the links between topics.
Linear	Linear (or terminal) assessment is carried out at the end of a study programme. Assessment covers the full qualification and provides a single opportunity for assessment. Critics highlight how linear assessment can be stressful and involves high stakes for learners as success all 'comes down to the day'.
Synoptic	Synoptic assessment requires learners to connect and combine knowledge, understanding and skills acquired in different parts of their qualification. This approach allows learners to increase their understanding in other parts of the programme, or across the programme as a whole. A holistic approach to coursework assessment is often taken, allowing learners to demonstrate a range of skills covered in different units or modules.

Changes have also been made to vocational assessment practice on many work-related qualifications. The Wolf Review of Vocational Education (2011) recommended that an element of external assessment be introduced to accredited vocational qualifications.

All those [awards] which are used, vocational or academic, should make serious demands of students, develop and accredit distinctive skills and attainments, facilitate progression post-16 and incorporate clearly established, and properly monitored, national standards. They must, therefore, have a strong element of external assessment. This need not, and indeed should not, mean assessment entirely on the basis of examinations, which in the case of vocational awards will often be quite inappropriate. But we know that, without regular external referencing, assessment standards in any subject invariably diverge across institutions and assessors. (Wolf, 2011: 112)

Wolf clearly points out that for many vocational qualifications, adding an examination may well not be the most appropriate way to ensure clearly established and properly maintained national standards. Many vocational qualifications are exploring other external assessment methods that ensure standards are maintained but which do not involve completing lengthy, written-based assessments in cold gym halls.

Reflection point

What do you think about Professor Wolf's call to ensure national standards are maintained through the introduction of external assessment? What other methods of external assessment are available to awarding organisations without resorting to traditional written examinations?

Whatever summative assessment methods are ultimately used, they should reflect the demands of the vocational area being taught. At what point again in employment will a learner be asked to sit in silence, alone, without any information or communication network to draw upon in order to recall and apply information? Perhaps a better form of assessment would be to assess learners' initiative, their digital literacy skills, how they are able to solve problems under pressure drawing on the resources around them, including the internet.

What do we want to assess?

Assessments are used for many different purposes in education. Two of the main reasons learners are assessed are to evaluate and improve individual learner performance and to audit or measure system performance (the performance of many learners across classrooms, schools, colleges, training providers, departments, authorities).

Depending on the subject and the timing of assessment, we may want to make judgements about individual learners':

- knowledge and understanding;
- technical and practical skills;
- functional skills: English, maths and ICT;
- general learning skills.

Individual assessments may focus on making judgements about one or many different skills at once. Assessment might be holistic and cover a range of assessment criteria which demonstrate learners' knowledge, understanding and skills. This is often an approach taken when assessing practical application.

How do we want to assess?

- **Tutor-led assessment:** where you as the tutor or assessor make judgements on the level of learners' performance and their competence.

- **Self-assessment:** where learners make their own judgement on their own levels of attainment.

- **Peer assessment:** where learners make assessment judgements of each other.

- **Computer-based assessments:** for example automated on-screen tests and exams that check learners' responses against the programmed correct answers.

Classroom and workshop assessment tools

Classroom assessment is concerned with the evaluation and improvement of individual learner performance and is highly contextualised to your specialised area and to the education experiences of learners within specific classrooms and workshops. Tutors and learners gain immediate and detailed feedback as to how effectively learners have learned the subject matter.

Many different assessment tools are available for tutors to use in the classroom or workshop:

- questioning;

- homework;

- projects;

- lab work;

- work-based scenarios;

- tests and quizzes;

- presentations (group and/or individual);

- reviews;

- reflective logs;

- essays and assignments;

- portfolios and electronic portfolios (e-Portfolios).

Each method can provide different learning opportunities and feedback for learners. As tutors selecting from these options, you evaluate which assessment is most appropriate for the purpose and the effect that assessment may have on student learning. For example, a building site workshop can be used to provide learners with a hands-on learning experience, as well as to assess the understanding learners have of the bricklaying principles involved in building a wall.

A writing exercise might be used to evaluate learners' technical abilities to write essays or research a paper, as well as their specific knowledge of an event, person, issue or future career plan.

Activity

Consider how your course materials promote effective assessment.

Types of assessment

Initial assessment

This is the process of assessing individual learners' needs, abilities, aptitudes, preferences and prior learning. A number of paper-based and online tools can help tutors to gather initial assessment information about their learning in order to plan learning. Initial assessment is explored in more detail in Chapter 5 on planning.

Diagnostic assessment

Diagnostic assessment is intended to improve the learners' experiences and their level of achievement. It assesses what the learners already know and the nature of difficulties (for example dyslexia) that they might have, which, if undiagnosed, might limit their engagement in new learning. It is often used before the programme commences and an individual learning plan (ILP) is put in place to address any development points.

Formative assessment

Formative assessment is an integral part of teaching and learning. It contributes to learning through providing timely feedback throughout the programme. It should indicate what is good about a piece of work and why this is good; it should also indicate what needs development and the strategies that need to be put in place to address this.

Remember effective formative feedback will affect what the learners and the tutor do next. It is a means to intervene to increase learning while encouraging learners to become more effective. In the process of developing deep understanding and reasoning, clear learning goals and effective communication shift the motivation for learning to the students. Learning becomes intrinsically motivating.

Activity

Consider how you use formative assessment to provide intrinsic motivation.

You may have considered that you will use concept maps to ascertain your learners' knowledge.

What are concept maps?
Concept maps are graphical tools for organising and representing knowledge. They include concepts, usually enclosed in bubbles, circles or boxes of some type, and relationships between concepts indicated by a connecting line or arrow linking two concepts. Words on the line or arrow, referred to as linking words or linking phrases, specify the relationship between the two concepts.

Summative assessment

Summative assessment demonstrates the extent of learners' success in meeting the assessment criteria used to measure the intended learning outcomes of a module or programme, and which contributes to the final mark given for the module. It is normally, though not always, used at the end of a unit of teaching. Summative assessment is used to quantify achievement, to reward achievement, to provide data for selection (to the next stage in education or to employment). For all these reasons the validity and reliability of summative assessment are of the greatest importance.

Remember the outcome of a summative assessment can be used formatively when learners take the results and use them to guide their efforts and activities in future courses.

Criterion referenced assessment

Each learner's achievement is judged against specific criteria. In principle no account is taken of how other learners have performed. Reliability and validity should be assured through processes such as internal quality assurance (IQA), moderation and verification, standardisation and the collation of exemplars in your subject-specific area. The vast majority of accredited vocational qualifications include a range of assessment criteria. These may be pass or fail where a learner needs to demonstrate a minimum level of competence, or they may be graduated to demonstrate a range of learner skills, for example Pass, Merit or Distinction.

Ipsative assessment

This is assessment measured against the learners' own previous standards. It can indicate how well a particular task has been undertaken against the learners' own average attainments, against their best work, or against their most recent piece of work. Ipsative assessment tends to correlate with effort, to promote effort-based attributions of success, and to enhance motivation to learn.

Activity

Consider a course you currently teach on.

- *How do the assessment methods align with the course learning outcomes?*
- *What kind of feedback would the learners receive and how would this contribute to their progress?*
- *Which functional skills and technologies would support this?*

Tutors have a professional responsibility to the learners to employ current and best practices in all facets of teaching and training, including assessment. Tutors want their learners to succeed and to achieve and yet, for many, the learning goals and content of assessments remain vague.

Remember involving the learners in the whole process of assessment gives clarity and direction to teaching and increases learners' motivation. Involving learners in assessing their own and each other's work gives the tutor greater insight into motivation and progress and is a source of valuable data for reporting to employers and parents.

Tips for effective assessment

- Provide choice and help learners to take responsibility and the lead for their learning.

- Discuss with learners the purpose of their learning and provide feedback that will help the learning process. Be explicit about what learning has taken place.

- Encourage learners to judge their work by how much they have learned and by the progress they have made.

- Facilitate learners' understanding of the criteria by which their learning is assessed and the assessment of their own work and that of their peers.

- Develop learners' understanding of the goals of their work in terms of what they are learning; provide feedback to learners in relation to these goals.

- Support learners to understand where they are in relation to learning goals and how to make further progress.

- Offer feedback that facilitates learners in knowing the next steps and how to succeed in taking them.

- Encourage learners to value effort and a wide range of attainments.

- Encourage collaboration among learners and respect for one another.

So what should you do less of?

- Define the curriculum in terms of what is in the tests to the detriment of what is not tested.

- Give frequent drill and practice for test-taking.

- Teach how to answer specific test questions.

- Allow test anxiety to impair some learners' performances.

- Use tests and assessment to tell learners where they are in relation to others.

- Give feedback relating to learners' capabilities, implying a fixed view of each learner's potential – lowering aspirations.

- Compare learners' grades and allow learners to compare grades, giving status on the basis of test achievement only.

- Isolate learners from the cycle of learning and teaching.

Julie is a swimming tutor working for a large private training provider.

For as long as my memory allows swimming qualifications have been assessed in a mostly academic way with the inclusion of exams. The externally assessed component was often technical in nature with learners wanting to stand up in the middle of an exam hall and demonstrate (which they were forbidden to do), and the job of describing in words what was happening in the water proved challenging to all. The standardisation of markers and the consistency of exam papers was another challenge with many learners not achieving well because although they were competent 'on poolside' they did not achieve well on the exam paper.

Anecdotally swimming has high numbers of dyslexic learners and the dominant learning and assessment styles are 'doers' ... those that loathe sitting still and revising! And of course to be a great tutor or coach involves about 5 per cent writing and remembering and 95 per cent doing on poolside. So the approach was not work related, did not enhance employability skills and would not fully translate to more medals in major games.

So in 2010 it all changed. With the advent of the Qualifications Credit Framework (QCF), the world of swimming assessment was modernised. Gone were the exams, replaced by criterion, pool-based assessment, involving progressive practical syllabi. Assessment is holistic to prevent duplication and repetition, with the use of recognition of prior learning (RPL) proving more and more popular. This allows learners to proactively use their prior experiences, documenting evidence from a broad range of sources. This means the largely unqualified pool-based experts (often parents and former competitive swimmers) with a lifelong dedication to the sport can be recognised for their expertise quickly and effectively. The practical and vocational aspects of teaching and learning should dictate the assessment methods, not the other way round. It is essential to align what you are teaching with how you teach and how you assess, otherwise there is a clear mismatch.

Feed-forward not back!

The power of feedback is highlighted in research as one of the most important roles of a tutor (Hattie, 2012). Good feedback can be very motivating but poor feedback can have the opposite effect, reducing confidence and threatening self-esteem. Rather than spending too much time and effort on reviewing the past and what learners cannot do, it may be more helpful to evaluate and highlight what learners can do and to provide guidance and clear targets on how they can improve and make better progress going forward.

The 'WWW' (What Went Well?) approach is often used alongside 'EBI' (Even Better If...) by colleagues in schools to highlight what learners need to do to improve. Black and Wiliam (1999) advocate a 'Medal and Mission' approach to feedback. Give your learners feedback on what they did well (the medal) and guidance on how to improve (the mission).

Table 7.2 Examples of WWW and EDI approaches

Feed-back The medal (What Went Well 'WWW')	Feed-forward The mission (Even Better If... EBI)
Well done Reena! You approached your customer service role-plays with commitment and enthusiasm. You were able to demonstrate how you met the needs of different customer types in different ways – on the telephone, face-to-face and in writing. You gave clear and appropriate responses to the dissatisfied customer who made a complaint. You demonstrated a clear understanding of the need to refer some matters to your supervisor if they are outside of your control. Your strategy for recording the key points of each customer enquiry really worked, although be careful with the accuracy of your written English. Very well done.	You have demonstrated sufficient knowledge, skills and understanding in order to achieve a Pass on this unit. To challenge yourself to achieve even further, you should: • proofread your written responses to customer enquiries, to ensure that your spelling and grammar are accurate and professional. This is very important when dealing with the general public. • develop your range of non-verbal communication skills, so you engage your customers with better eye contact and do not demonstrate 'closed' body language. You might find the video clip on the VLE useful in outlining some strategies to practise here.

Reinforcing a 'growth mindset' through feedback

The way that we provide feedback and praise can reinforce a growth or fixed mindset perspective in our learners. For example, offering praise that is person-focused, e.g. 'you are very good at that task', reinforces that a learners' ability is fixed. If their performance in the next task is not so good, what does this mean if their ability is set? This can lead to a great deal of pressure and a temptation to avoid making mistakes and challenges to minimise the risk of failure.

Instead, try to offer process-orientated praise which focuses on learners' levels of effort, engagement, approach and motivation. For example, 'the way you approached the group task was efficient and productive, which led to great results'. This approach helps learners to make connections between their approach to learning and their level of progress and achievement, giving them the confidence and skills to approach new and more challenging situations, tasks and projects.

Learners who develop a growth mindset will be better prepared to deal with making mistakes. They will see a fail as a 'first attempt at learning' and not a reflection on their level of intelligence. With self-esteem intact, growth mindset learners will be more resilient to overcome challenges and seek out problems to solve.

F – First

A – Attempt

I – In

L – Learning

Consider a recent activity you completed with your learners or the feedback you provided on a piece of assessed work. What praise and feedback did you offer? Was it person- or process-orientated?

Identify three ways that you might frame your learner feedback in a way that supports a growth mindset approach.

Questioning

The development of sound questioning skills should be a key aim of any vocational tutor. Questioning can be a most effective way of providing a differentiated and personalised assessment strategy which requires minimal preparation.

A range of different question types can be utilised, including:

- open;
- closed;
- general;
- nominated;
- probing;
- differentiated;
- written or verbal;
- peer questioning.

Open questions are usually more effective at drawing out learners' thoughts, perceptions, understanding and opinions than closed questions, which promote a specific, set or limited response.

How can you develop your questioning technique further? Do you differentiate your questioning approach to provide each learner with an 'optimal' level of challenge'?

The assignment brief

For many work-related qualifications, learning providers are encouraged to create and design their own assessment tool, often known as an 'assignment brief'. The brief provides a link between what the learners are required to do (the assessment criteria) and how they are to demonstrate their level of knowledge, understanding and skills to meet the demands of each criterion.

Typically, good assignment briefs should:

- provide clear tasks that will allow learners to produce authentic evidence to meet the assessment criteria;

- give learners clear guidance as to what they are required to do;

- outline the time available to complete the assessment tasks;

- feature a vocational scenario to contextualise the tasks to a specific sector or industry;

- allow learners to generate evidence in a range of different formats to meet their styles and preferences (where appropriate), for example reports, posters, websites, presentations and multimedia evidence.

Activity

Review the example assignment brief in Figure 7.1. Evaluate the advantages and disadvantages of its design. What would you do differently when designing your own summative assessment tool?

Level 2 Vocationally Related Qualification (VRQ) in Travel and Tourism

Unit 4: Customer Service: Assignment Task 1

Issue date:

Interim deadline:

Final deadline:

Scenario

Beacon
Hotel

Hotels attract a variety of customer types including domestic and overseas visitors, guests staying for leisure and business purposes and those with specific and special needs. It is most important that all guests receive excellent customer service throughout their visit. Many hotels employ a range of full-time, part-time and casual employees and it is important that all staff members are trained properly in order to deliver a consistently high level of customer service.

(Continued)

Figure 7.1   An example vocational assignment brief

Continued

You are required to complete a number of activities that are related to the importance and delivery of customer service in a hotel, reflecting on and reviewing your own performance and identifying opportunities for improvements.

Task 1 *(LO.1.1, LO.1.2, LO.1.3, LO.2.1, LO.3.1)*

Staff working in travel and tourism organisations need to know what customer service is, why it is so important to all travel and tourism businesses and the impact that legislation and controls have on customer service delivery.

You are required to create an information resource for new staff that have been recruited to work at a local three-star hotel – Beacon Hotel.

The resource should:

- Describe how the diverse needs of different customers are **identified** and **met.**

- Describe the different methods and media used to communicate effectively with **internal** and **external** customers.

- Describe the impact of **personal presentation** on customer **perception** of the travel and tourism sector.

- Explain the impact of **excellent** and **poor** customer service on business success.

- Explain the impact of key **legislation** on customer service delivery to internal and external customers, using appropriate examples to support and illustrate your explanation.

Your information resource could, for example, be an induction booklet, training video or customer service podcast for new staff. You may choose to use more than one method of presenting your information. Your tutor will give you further guidance on the best presentation method.

Task 2 *(LO.4.1, LO.4.2, LO.4.3, LO.5.1, LO.5.2)*

The hotel's general manager would like a new member of staff to observe you communicating effectively with customers. After taking part in a number of different practice role-play scenarios, your tutor will take the role of the new member of staff and will formally observe you participating in one selected customer service situation. You should demonstrate your ability to:

- identify and respond to diverse customer needs;

- use different communication methods and media;

- comply with customer service standards, legislation and controls.

Your tutor will complete an Observation Record of your performance.

It is important for those delivering customer services in the travel and tourism sector to review and assess their own performance so they can identify improvements for the future.

Following on from your practice and formal role-play customer service situations, you are now required to:

- review and evaluate your performance in delivering customer service satisfaction against agreed standards;

- propose solutions for improvement of the customer experience that could benefit others as well as yourself.

Your performance review could be in the form of a written report, reflective log or video diary, or a combination of methods. Your tutor will provide you with further guidance on the best way for you to present your evidence.

Case study

Catherine is a lecturer in business studies in a FE college.

I am a successful business lecturer and course team leader for Level 2 and Level 3 BTEC Business. I teach across a range of full- and part-time day and evening courses to learners from Level 1 through to degree level, including employability short courses. I have 17 years' industrial experience in retailing and learning and development. I have a wealth of experience in training and developing people across a wide range of ages and from varying backgrounds and experiences. This has included one-to-one coaching, group delivery, wide audience presentations and the design and development of work-based learning curriculums.

I draw on this experience to enhance the learning for my students. Vocational business learners often come to me and say 'I just want to get a good job and this course can help me do that'. These words are at the heart of everything I do. I feel I have the responsibility of preparing them for working life. No matter what route that may take, there are skills, or as the business world would call them, 'competencies,' that learners will need to develop not just to get that job in business but to go on to have a successful career.

Rather than descriptive tasks that match the criteria definitions of 'describe', 'explain' and 'compare', I devise assignments that require learners to carry out activities that evidence that these criteria have been achieved, for example, by producing a factsheet for new small businesses on the financial factors to consider when setting up a business. Learners need to research all the factors,

(Continued)

(Continued)

identify the relevant ones for a small business and then comprehend them enough to give a summary description. Putting things in a factsheet can be harder than simply describing it!

This approach allows you to work through several levels of Bloom's taxonomy. It minimises the lengthy descriptive writing that learners tire of. The time and effort is in the journey to producing the work and not necessarily the final work. It helps develop the softer skills that will better equip the learner for the real world of work.

Learners are often challenged by this approach. It can be uncomfortable for them at times, but I have found that at the end of their course they have developed more responsibility for their learning by operating in an environment that resembles real working life. More and more exam bodies are supportive of different approaches to assessment. Reflective logs, observations, video evidence are all actively encouraged.

With not only more creativity being allowed for in assessment but also in curriculum design, we have a responsibility as the instruments of learning to take the opportunities in front of us to enrich vocational teaching. This can be challenging for tutors. Time constraints, administration and organisational cultures can be challenging. However, I accept the challenge. Business tutors need to draw on a range of soft skills themselves in order to create learners with those skills. We need to be entrepreneurial in order to create entrepreneurs. After all, working in an ambiguous environment and sometimes not knowing what is coming next are real-life challenges that develop not only the learner but the tutor too!

Activity

Having read Catherine's case study, consider the assessment tasks that you design and how the skills required to be successful support the skills required in industry.

Choosing the right assessment tools

In carrying out your assessments, it is important that you are familiar with the tools you will be using. Your assessment tools give shape and form to your chosen assessment method. They must, therefore, be fit for purpose. You need to fully consider which tool is needed to most meaningfully, effectively and efficiently support your chosen assessment method. As identified in Chapter 5 you should also be aware of and take into account the language, literacy and numeracy skill level of the learners and the requirements of the units of competency when you design your tool.

How can you ensure that you feel confident to utilise the tools?

- Be clear about the mandatory requirements of the assessment tasks.

- Apply your understanding of the specified competencies to choose appropriate assessment methods.

- Spend time creating meaningful assessment tools – this may be in conjunction with colleagues and learners.

- Pilot your tools to help you fully develop your confidence that the tools can be used meaningfully, flexibly and support you to make valid, reliable and fair judgements.

Assessment planning

It is often useful, and sometime a requirement, to complete an assessment plan which outlines how the learning outcomes and assessment criteria of a particular study pro-gramme will be achieved within the timeframe available. An assessment plan template (see Appendix 2) can help course teams to identify how and when individual units and modules will be assessed, including:

- Assignment brief issue date – when the assignment is given to learners.

- Deadline for interim submission deadline and issuing of formative feedback.

- Deadline for final submission and issuing of summative feedback.

- Dates for internal verification of assessment decisions.

Activity

Use the assessment plan template in Appendix 2 to help you consider how and when you will assess a specific study programme.

Summary

In this chapter you have learnt about:

- *why, what and how to assess vocational learners;*

- *modular, linear and synoptic assessment;*

- *initial, formative and summative assessment;*

- *writing vocational assignment briefs;*

- *giving feedback.*

Theory focus

Further reading

Bloxham, S and Boyd, P (2007) *Developing Effective Assessment in Higher Education: A Practical Guide.* Berkshire: Open University Press.

Duckworth, V and White, C (2009) *On the Job: Car Mechanic Tutor Resources CD-Rom.* Warrington: Gatehouse Media Limited.

Dweck, C (2012) *Mindset: How You Can Fulfil Your Potential.* London: Robinson Publishing.

Gravells, A (2012) *Preparing to Teach in the Lifelong Learning Sector.* London: Learning Matters/SAGE.

Ofqual (2009) *Authenticity – A Guide for Teachers.* Coventry: Ofqual.

Petty, G (2009) *Teaching Today: A Practical Guide* (Fourth Edition). Nelson Thornes.

Scales, P (2013) *Teaching in the Lifelong Learning Sector.* Maidenhead: Open University Press.

Tummons, J (2011) *Assessing Learning in the Lifelong Learning Sector* (Third Edition). London: Learning Matters/SAGE.

Wood, J and Dickinson, J (2001) *Quality Assurance and Evaluation in the Lifelong Learning Sector.* Exeter: Learning Matters.

Websites

Joint Council of Qualifications (JCQ): www.jcq.org.uk

Ofqual: www.ofqual.gov.uk

References

Black, P and Wiliam, D (1999) *Assessment for Learning: Beyond the Black Box.* Cambridge: University of Cambridge School of Education.

Hattie, J. (2012) *Visible Learning for Teachers, Maximising Impact on Learning.* Oxford: Routledge.

Wolf, A (2011) *Review of Vocational Education – The Wolf Report.* London: The Stationery Office.

8 OBSERVING VOCATIONAL LEARNING

In this chapter you will learn about:

- e-Portfolios and personal development records;
- using online applications to store and record learner evidence;
- the importance of authentic and reliable evidence;
- plagiarism and malpractice;
- observation records and witness testimonies.

Professional Standards

Standard 9: Assess learner achievement – KU13 How to record and store assessment decisions, who they should be made available to and the data protection and confidentiality guidelines that should be followed

Standard 11: Internally monitor and maintain the quality of assessment – KU13 Procedures to follow when there are concerns about the quality of assessment: when and how to use them

Standard 12: Externally monitor and maintain the quality of assessment – KU1 The key concepts and principles of assessment

Standard 13: Evaluate and improve learning and development provision – KU9 The contribution that technology can make to the monitoring and evaluation process

Introduction

Having explored the main principles of assessment in Chapter 7, this chapter explores issues around the recording of evidence. As many vocational qualifications seek to develop learners' working competences in a given employment sector or industry, much assessment (both formative and summative) is likely to be of learners demonstrating their practical skills. Evidence of learners' skills could be recorded in a number of different ways:

- through multimedia evidence recordings – such as audio and video;

- through an assessors' confirmation of the learners' skills documented in observation records;

- through an employers' expert testimony of the learners' competences and skills;

- through the learners' own reflections and evaluations of their skills and competencies.

A range of different forms of evidence is usually required to provide sufficient evidence that all the required assessment criteria have been met and the learner is able to demonstrate a sufficient level of knowledge, understanding and skill to meet the national standards required.

Evidence of this standard is often collated in the form of a portfolio, electronic portfolio (e-Portfolio) or professional development records.

Portfolios and Personal Development Records (PDR)

When in college or on work placement your learners can try to capture, record and reflect on their progress through a personal development record (PDR). The record can help learners to monitor and record their progress and develop their independent learning skills. The PDR can also include other learning achievements, both in the course of their subject-specific area and in activities related to it, for example assignments that link theory to practice, as well as practical demonstration of skills competence. The personal development record is often designed and submitted as a portfolio of evidence, which may be paper-based, electronic or online.

Paper-based portfolios do not require any IT equipment or digital skill to compile but the amount of evidence and tracking required on many vocational programmes can often lead to very comprehensive portfolios which are difficult to manage. Evidence is also precious and many hours of effort and hard work will have gone into its compilation. If the portfolio is lost or stolen, this can have serious consequences for many months or even years of study.

e-Portfolios

For many learners and tutors, the development of online or electronic portfolios (e-Portfolios) can be a better way of collecting, collating, managing and sharing assessment evidence. Many e-Portfolios are commercial products that may have been bought by your employer or learning organisation. Other options include the use of free, web-based (or cloud-based) tools available on the internet.

Unlike a traditional paper-based portfolio, learners can easily upload and integrate multimedia evidence, such as video and audio material, in an e-Portfolio. Hyperlinks can be made to other resources also online, for example blogs, reflections and YouTube videos. E-Portfolios allow evidence to be structured, organised and mapped against specific topics, modules and assessment criteria. This can help learners to develop organisational skills, take control of their learning and track their progress and assessment.

Many e-Portfolios provide a structured framework for the presentation and organisation of learner evidence, mapped against specific assessment criteria, for example, those found in NVQ and BTEC qualifications. It is always worth checking what your organisational policy is on recording evidence, data protection, the use of electronic tools and issues of security and storage.

We identify (Ingle and Duckworth, 2013), various applications that are freely available from Google which are becoming an increasingly popular way of providing free and sustainable e-Portfolio capabilities. A range of Google apps are available, including:

- Google Sites: for the presentation of web content, including media-rich resources as a linked portfolio of online evidence.

- Google Calendar: for arranging, sharing and tracking events and appointments.

- Google Talk: for online calls or for sending instant messages.

- Google Drive: allows learners and practitioners to create, share and store documents, spreadsheets, and presentations. Google Drive also facilitates real-time collaboration to allow multiple learners to work on creating documents together.

- Google Groups: to create manageable spaces to keep related documents, web content and other information in one place.

- Google Video for education: for video hosting and sharing.

Other popular tools for the storage and presentation of information, material and resources include Drop Box (www.dropbox.com) and Evernote (www.evernote.com) where users can upload their files for secure storage online. Learners and tutors are able to share documents such as assignments with each other. Mobile applications (apps) are also available to upload and share evidence on the go.

Whichever method of recording and storage is used, learner-produced evidence recorded and stored in portfolios should be authentic, valid and reliable.

Authentic evidence

The evidence in learners' PDPs should relate either to work they have completed or be statements about them from people, for example, their workplace mentor or supervisor. To improve the level of authenticity, the PDPs could include photographs of skills being demonstrated. Signed declarations of authenticity should also feature, where learners confirm that the evidence they are submitting is original and their own work. For most qualifications, this is a specific requirement and must be completed if the evidence is to be seen as valid.

Reliable evidence

The evidence should represent the consistent standard of their work. The evidence should also be reliable in the sense that statements about their work should come from reliable witnesses who will be honest, independent and objective. Using witness testimonies for learners' friends at work or from those who are not suitably qualified or experienced in the vocational area will generally not been seen as reliable forms of evidence and may well be rejected by the internal and external verifier or moderator.

Plagiarism and malpractice

The Joint Council for Qualifications (JCQ, 2012) defines plagiarism as *[t]he failure to acknowledge sources properly and/or the submission of another person's work as if it were the candidate's own.*

For most learners, this may mean copying work from the internet or textbooks without citing the work, or copying from other learners. Although cases of plagiarism are quite possible in all forms of assessment, the use of coursework and portfolios of evidence gives more opportunities for learners to submit evidence of knowledge, skills and understanding that are not authentic.

Many higher education institutions are using sophisticated plagiarism detection software, such as Turnitin (www.turnitin.com), to deter learners from submitting evidence that has been downloaded from online sources or copied from other learners.

To try to get around such advances, there has been an increase in the number of learners 'commissioning' original pieces of assessment evidence from other people. As the evidence has not been directly copied from existing sources, detection software is often incapable of highlighting it as non-authentic. Tutors should be vigilant and aware of such practices and ensure that assignment briefs and assessment tools are designed with care to include tasks and activities that are difficult to commission from others. Such tasks could include individual presentations, working with real clients over time on a project activity and other practical tasks that require a direct observation of practice.

The Joint Council of Qualifications (JCQ, 2012: 3) defines malpractice (which includes maladministration) as any act, default or practices which:

- compromises, attempts to compromise or may compromise the process of assessment, the integrity of any qualification or the validity of a result or certificate; and/or

- damages the authority, reputation or credibility of any awarding body or centre or any officer, employee or agent of any awarding body or centre.

Malpractice may be committed by tutors and learners and covers a range of issues, including:

- plagiarism;

- breaches of security;

- deceptions;

- improper assistance to candidates;

- maladministration;

- collusion;

- making a false declaration of authenticity.

Activity

Most organisations will have clear policies and procedures in place for dealing with suspected cases of malpractice and plagiarism. Find out what your organisational procedure is and what your responsibilities are.

Creating a learning log

The learning log is essentially a diary or journal of events in which learners can record their reactions to them. It tends to be a snapshot of their current, on-going thinking as opposed to later reflection.

A learning log may include signposts to questions you want your learners to address, for example:

- What is significant about the lesson?

- What could have been handled differently?

- What have you learned?

Many learners may prefer to keep their learning logs online or through electronic methods. Blogs (short for weblogs) can provide a convenient and accessible way for learners to document their on-going learning experiences.

Recording and evidencing practical skills

Many vocational qualifications require learners to demonstrate a given level and standard of skills and competences. These are often assessed through direct observation by the tutor or a dedicated assessor, through simulated or real practical activities. This could include assessing:

- the hairdressing learner completing a specific cut on a client in a commercial salon;

- the hospitality student serving diners in the college training restaurant;

- the health and social care learner meeting the needs of their elderly clients in a care home setting;

- the floristry learner dressing an events hall for a special occasion;

- the travel and tourism learner performing a safety demonstration in a mock aircraft cabin;

- the business administration learner scanning confidential documents in a busy office environment.

A range of evidence could be collected to support an assessment judgement that the learners are competent and skilled to carry out these duties in line with the assessment criteria and national occupational standards. Evidence could include:

- photographs;

- video;

- professional discussions;

- reflections;

- observation records;

- expert witness testimony.

Rather than relying on one single piece of evidence, providing a range of evidence to confirm the learners' skills better supports a valid and reliable assessment judgement.

Observation records and witness testimonies

An observation record is typically completed by a tutor or assessor who has direct knowledge of the specification in order for an accurate assessment decision to be made. The record is used to provide a formal record of the assessment judgement based on the learner's performance. The record should:

- record the assessor's clear and detailed comments;

- be referenced against the specific assessment criteria being assessed, which are found in the relevant qualification specification;

- be individual to a specific learner;

- be sufficiently detailed to enable others to make a judgement as to quality and whether there is sufficient evidence of performance;

- confirm that national standards have been achieved (if appropriate);

- be accompanied by supporting/additional evidence, such as presentation notes, photo graphs, learning log;

- be signed and dated by both the assessor and the learner.

A witness testimony is typically completed by someone other than the tutor or assessor of the qualification but who is able to make a professional judgement about the performance of the learner in the given situation.

A witness may be a learner's supervisor at work or on work placement, a technician, learning support assistant or manager. The witness must have seen the learner demonstrating their performance against the specific criteria being assessed and be given clear guidance on the desirable characteristics required for the learner to be successful in their skills performance.

An observation record has greater validity than a witness testimony as it directly records an assessment decision. A witness testimony cannot confer an assessment decision, as the witness is not the trained tutor or assessor. Witness testimonies provide valuable supporting evidence of learners' skills and performance but they should not be the only or main form of assessment evidence.

Ethics and evidence

Evidence can also be in the form of photographs, video or audio recording. Digital video and accompanying editing software are increasingly becoming more accessible to teachers in terms of ease of use and cost. There are however ethical considerations in photographing, audio and video-recording of workplace practices. It is important that informed consent is given to carry out the above and in the case of a minor this needs to be given by the parents or carers.

Observation record

Qualification:	VRQ Hospitality		**Centre Number:**	X123456
Unit number & title:	The Customer Experience		**Location of observation:**	Training room
Learner's UCI:	000123555		**Date:**	02 November
Learner's name:	Reena Padayachee		**Learner's signature:**	*Reena*

Description of activity undertaken

The learner carried out a role-play scenario. The tutor acted as the businessperson.

Scenario: *You are a receptionist at a successful hotel and restaurant. You have just checked in a customer (a businessperson) who has travelled a long way. The businessperson is angry and tells you that the room is cold and dirty.*

A script was written by the learner as preparation for how they expected the conversation to develop. The learner practised variations on the script with friends or family members. The learner was keen to incorporate agreed standards for dealing with complaints into the role-play and using a script as preparation facilitated this.

Describe how the learner met each criteria and the qualitative aspects of their performance

LO1 – Throughout the role-play Reena's attitude was friendly, sympathetic and helpful. Reena quickly established what the complaint was about and reassured the customer that she would do her best to resolve the problem. When the customer complained about his time being wasted Reena changed her plan and offered the customer an immediate upgrade to his room, which he accepted. Reena identified and responded to the customer's needs appropriately (Merit 1).

(Continued)

(Continued)

LO2 – Reena greeted the customer in a professional way as she approached reception with open gestures and a smile. Reena had prepared for the role-play by dressing in a smart business suit, to create the right impression. She listened to the customer and remained calm despite his anger. Whilst the role-play was taking place Reena kept the customer regularly informed of progress. She demonstrated appropriate use of different communication methods – verbal and non-verbal. Well done! (Merit 2).

LO3 – The customer complaint was dealt with effectively and quickly. Reena used agreed standards for dealing with a complaint effectively (e.g. she had learned about the complaints policy during a visit to a large local hotel and used this framework during the role-play). The complaint was dealt with internally to the customer's satisfaction so the involvement of lawyers and subsequent legislation was not necessary on this occasion. Reena complied with customer service standards and controls in an effective way (Merit 3).

Overall Reena, you have demonstrated your skills in meeting all the criteria to national standards. I was very impressed by the professional way you approached this scenario – very well done.

Assessor signature: _____

Learner signature: _____

Date: _____

Figure 8.1   An example skills observation record

Witness testimony

Learner name:	
Qualification:	
Unit number and title:	
Description of activity undertaken – *include where, when and how*	
Assessment criteria for which the activity provides evidence – *list specific criteria if known*	
Judge how the activity meets the requirements of the assessment criteria – *the quality of performance*	

Witness name and job role:			
Witness signature:		Date:	
Learner name:			
Learner signature:		Date:	
Assessor name:			
Assessor signature:		Date:	

Figure 8.2   An example witness testimony pro forma

Case study

Claire is a tutor of Early Years education at a private training provider.

To ensure the maintenance of standards, the training provider I work for has an internal and external structure of professionals that it liaises with to support, monitor and collect data to verify that the recording of assessment is valid and reliable and that the learner's evidence is authentic, i.e. created by them. The quality process complies with the requirements of the awarding organisation and the regulator (Ofqual).

The policy and procedure for quality assurance in my organisation identifies and stipulates the requirement that all members of staff must be compliant, including being up to date with the new Training Assessment and Quality Assurance qualification (TAQA).

We also have to demonstrate that we understand the national occupational standards, processes of the awarding body and maintain accurate records of internal quality assurance (IQA). As part of continual professional development (CPD), achievement of these requirements has to be documented.

The Institute for Learning's (IfL) code of professional practice is reflected throughout the IQA policies and strategy.

Learners' portfolios are checked and 'sampled' at various stages throughout their course. This is to check that tutors and assessors are demonstrating valid, reliable and fair assessments of learners' work. The outcome of these checks improves practice for the future and allows tutors to share good practice and develop new ideas and strategies. For example, I used the IQA report to develop a group activity for teaching and assessing child development, using a digital camera to photograph learners' work as evidence for their portfolios.

Sampling learners' portfolios is completed at intermittent times throughout the year and recorded by the Quality Assurance Co-ordinator (QAC) on a report form that the external standards verifier inspects.

My employer prides itself on keeping up to date with changes in the FE and Skills sector. All assessors have now completed their TAQA awards and this helps to ensure that staff practice remains current and within the new guidelines for assessment of learners' knowledge and competences.

Activity

In the case study above Claire identifies a number of different factors involved with assuring the quality and authenticity of vocational assessment evidence. How do you ensure the evidence of your learners is valid, reliable and authentic? Who is in charge of the internal quality assurance process in your organisation and what part do you play in the quality cycle?

Summary

In this chapter you have learnt about:

- *e-Portfolios and personal development records;*
- *using online applications to store and record learner evidence;*
- *the importance of authentic and reliable evidence;*
- *plagiarism and malpractice;*
- *observation records and witness testimonies.*

Theory focus

Further reading

Gravells, A (2012) *Preparing to Teach in the Lifelong Learning Sector*. London: Learning Matters/SAGE.

Ingle, S and Duckworth, V (2013) *Enhancing Learning through Technology in Lifelong Learning: Fresh Ideas; Innovative Strategies.* Maidenhead: Open University Press.

Ofqual (2009) *Authenticity – A Guide for Teachers*. Coventry: Ofqual.

Tummons, J (2011) *Assessing Learning in the Lifelong Learning Sector* (Third Edition). London: Learning Matters/SAGE.

Wood, J and Dickinson, J (2001) *Quality Assurance and Evaluation in the Lifelong Learning Sector*. Exeter: Learning Matters.

Websites

Joint Council of Qualifications (JCQ): www.jcq.org.uk

Ofqual: www.ofqual.gov.uk

DropBox: www.dropbox.com

Evernote: www.evernote.com

Google Drive: www.google.com/drive

PebblePad: www.pebblepad.com

References

Ingle, S and Duckworth, V (2013) *Enhancing Learning through Technology in Lifelong Learning: Fresh Ideas; Innovative Strategies.* Maidenhead: Open University Press.

JCQ (Joint Council for Qualifications) (2012) *General and Vocational Qualifications Suspected Malpractice in Examinations and Assessments: Policies and Procedures.* London: Joint Council for Qualifications.

9 THE PRACTITIONER VOICE

In this chapter you will learn about:

• good practice for new and experienced tutors in the FE and Skills sector.

Professional Standards

Standard 10: *Reflect on, develop and maintain own skills and practice in learning and Development*

Standard 13: *Evaluate and improve learning and development provision* – KU17 The impact of the wider learning environment on the learner experience

Introduction

In each chapter, we have unpicked and explored different aspects of vocational education within the context of the FE and Skills sector. This context is broad and many readers may also be teaching vocational education programmes in the compulsory school sector or in higher education settings.

We hope that each chapter has provided some areas for reflection, consideration and action planning as you build on your existing knowledge and experiences. We very much support a vision of excellent, high quality vocational programmes that offer all learners better and more successful futures for themselves and their families.

In this chapter, we draw together all the themes of planning, engaging employers, integrating and developing skills and designing assessment opportunities that allow learners to showcase their skills and achievements as they apply their learning. We present a range of case studies from excellent practitioners, both new and experienced, who share their approaches to vocational education and training.

These practitioners provide a valuable insight into their own vocational backgrounds and the strategies they use as 'dual professionals' to craft rich, experiential learning experiences for their diverse range of learners. We invite you to engage with their stories and consider what you might take from each as they share good practice and model approaches that might fit into your tutor's toolkits.

Drawing on the Ofsted *Common Inspection Framework for Learning and Skills* (2012), these case studies offer you expertise to ensure that on your vocational programme:

- learners benefit from high expectations, engagement, care, support and motivation from staff;

- staff use their skills and expertise to plan and deliver teaching, learning and support to meet each learner's needs;

- staff initially assess learners' starting points and monitor their progress, set challenging tasks, and build on and extend learning for all learners;

- learners understand how to improve as a result of frequent, detailed and accurate feedback from staff following assessment of their learning;

- teaching and learning develop English, mathematics and functional skills, and support the achievement of learning goals and career aims;

- appropriate and timely information, advice and guidance support learning effectively;

- equality and diversity are promoted through teaching and learning.

Finally, we invite you to reflect on each chapter of this book and consider your next steps for your practice. How will you raise the profile of vocational education, how will you promote a growth mindset in your learners, and how will you ensure the learning experiences you offer are inclusive, challenging and engaging for all?

Case study

Erica is a trainee Health and Social Care tutor working in the FE and training sector

My vocational background began as a mortgage advisor in a bank. A key part of my role was training and mentoring colleagues. During this period my strengths of supporting and delivering informative and motivating training sessions were repeatedly identified. Whilst enjoying my role I felt unfulfilled as a person and my journey to teach began when I enrolled on a Level 3 teaching assistant course. As part of the course I commenced a placement in a primary school. The volunteering role ignited my passion and creativity, further motivating me to begin my long, enjoyable yet 'unmapped' journey into teaching. Shortly after I had finished my teaching assistant course I sought employment in a diverse and challenging primary where I spent the next five years. During this time, I completed a foundation degree in Early Years and Children in Integrated Practice. This route into teaching allowed me to continue to work full time and care for my young family. Whilst not a traditional route to gain a degree and achieve QTLS it allowed me to gain practical experience in a range of settings and to identify my strengths. Studying whilst working and raising a family was a difficult one with many tears, bottles of wine and good friendships along the way.

After completing my foundation degree I enrolled at a local university to study a BA Hons Leadership and Management in Children's Services and achieved a First Hons. Again, I worked full time as a Cover Supervisor in a primary school, covering non-contact time for tutors within Key Stage 2 and delivering whole-school interventions. Whilst working I took on many additional roles including ICT Co-ordinator, Literacy Intervention Co-ordinator and mentoring support staff. During this time I identified my strengths and enjoyment of teaching adult learners and facilitating my knowledge. After a long four-year journey I graduated and left my job to pursue my dream of teaching. I enrolled on the PGCE PCET course and I am currently studying full time whilst completing a placement at a local college teaching Health and Social Care.

Throughout my teaching I ensure that I make links to the workplace and that opportunities are given for learners to relate theory to practice. The course entails the students completing placements, therefore I ensure learners seek placements that are able to support their professional development. In addition, I plan for a guest speaker input – from the relevant vocational sector; this has been very effective and learner feedback has been extremely positive.

I ensure my teaching methods inspire and motivate learners, allowing them to see the course as a journey. I ensure that the methods I use complement the learning styles of the learners. On a daily basis I challenge myself within the classroom to ensure I deliver lessons that engage and motivate learners.

I provide information through a variety of media – video, board, paper, work-book, actual demonstration, verbal explanation, questions and answers and practical activity.

I ensure that technology is at the heart of all my lessons, allowing learners to be inspired by new and emerging technology. For example, I delivered a lesson where learners use an iPad to download an app and do the grocery shopping for the service user they had been caring for.

I plan my lessons focusing on a spiral curriculum. At the start of every lesson I use Animoto to recap previous learning and I have involved learners in preparing the Animoto for the next lesson to ensure learning has taken place. Practice and repetition help to ensure that the learning undertaken is remembered and the meta-language is reinforced at the start of each session with all learners building their own dictionary of meta-language.

I plan lessons with lesson aims and objectives that allow learners to achieve the module outcomes whilst enriching their wider understanding and development.

I have invited nurses into the sessions when discussing the importance of hand-washing. Learners then had a practical lesson on the importance of hand-washing and prevention of disease within a care environment.

(Continued)

(Continued)

I have used case studies from the media to generate debate and asked the learners to participate in a blog to record their opinions. This has then formed part of their assessment and allowed me to check for learning at the end of each session.

The college has recently become a 'Centre for Excellence'. This has allowed the college to purchase hospital equipment that is used within the taught sessions to gain practical experience.

I have used and will continue to use guest speakers that I have built relationships with via networking over my five years in education. This also allows me to call upon their expertise when planning lessons. Trips have been arranged to visit hospital wards and care homes that link to units the learners have been studying.

In my experience the challenges learners face currently within health and social care are securing career opportunities. At times this has affected learners' motivation; also some learners fail to seek placement opportunities, therefore when linking theory to practice they have limited experience.

In addition, learners have increasingly busy lives and, with the cuts in funding due to the economic climate, learners have sought employment opportunities to replace the EMA. From this, some learners have already experienced the negative aspects of the job market and this can impact upon their belief that education is a powerful tool that can change their prospects. From very early on in their journey they begin to question the course and how it will change their life.

My approach to vocational teaching and learning encompasses a person-centred approach that allows autonomous learning. I encourage learners to use real-life experiences within the classroom and likewise I bring elements of my own experiences and life into the classroom.

Case study

Simon and Beth are directors of a non-profit equine training organisation. As experienced vocational tutors, they share some of their approaches to making learning engaging and effective, linked to aspects of the Ofsted Common Inspection Framework.

Ensure learners make good progress

A useful activity to set during induction week or to check prior learning is to set the learners a timed assessment (for example to strip and clean tack in five minutes). The tutor should record their progress initially, and then repeat the task later in the term, each time recording and assessing their progress against their previous times.

Peer assessment also works here, and you can even add an element of competition by rewarding the most improved learner with a prize. This task also works by introducing a quality element (as opposed to simply completing the task against the clock) after the initial few attempts, so that the tutor can help learners develop wider skills.

Another activity to check on-going progress is to set learners a series of increasingly difficult tasks (i.e. jumping poles at certain heights, which are then raised at subsequent attempts, depending on rates of progress) to show improvements from first attempt to last. Where learners are improving at different levels, ensure that they are tracked and the difficulty of tasks is appropriate for each learner (or group).

Learning takes place, both in and outside of the classroom

A good way of taking learning out of the classroom or yard could be to ask learners to draft a questionnaire that helps them identify a particular element of their course, for example, 'Who is a typical horse owner?' using their peers or members of public at a local show or event. Learners should be asked to record their findings (or create a log) and create a guidebook for prospective horse owners, once they have evaluated and condensed the information gathered.

Learners could be asked to video their dressage tests (or compete using Dressage Anywhere – a popular online dressage service) during time out of the college, and post their videos to the class Moodle pages, for peers to comment upon and help them improve their scores.

Setting high expectations

A common issue amongst practical learners is the ability to identify and develop the skills of their chosen profession whilst in a college environment, without it appearing patronising. Early on in the course, ask learners to research the standards and rules found and expected on professional yards (including health and safety) and then agree to negotiate a personal/class set of standards with the tutor. These should be drafted into a set of yard rules, together with any agreed consequences of breaches (the tutor should also agree to abide by these rules) and have them posted around the yard.

When confident of the standards, ask the learners to 'police' themselves during class-based and practical sessions, and the tutor can then arrange for regular reviews of behaviours, and oversee any emerging issues or consequences that fall short of the standards. Consistency of good behaviour is the key to this task, and having guest speakers from well-managed yards or industry is also a useful addition to this activity.

Innovative and inspired teaching strategies

Practical learners are often keen to develop their business and entrepreneurial skills, especially when television shows such as The Apprentice and

(Continued)

(Continued)

Dragons' Den are broadcast. When they have settled into the course set them an assignment that requires them to research the requirements of running a sustainable and successful yard (arranging trips to professionally run yards etc. is a good idea before setting this task). Then ask the learners to set up their own riding school or grooming service (i.e. for one afternoon on campus each week), for the other learners (or tutors/public).

Using their career goals, skill development targets or personal ambitions, the tutor should allocate admin roles and provide the group with a set budget to administer. The tutor should also draw up a negotiated 'contract' for the learners to sign to remind them of the professional standards they will need to adhere to, as well as the teamwork required.

Wider skills could include interviewing (for 'staffing'), marketing, health and safety, finance, web design and people management. At regular intervals, the tutor should monitor and support the learners' progress. Where possible the tutor should also reduce their input as the learners grow in confidence and professionalism and set SMART targets and milestones as the task progresses towards a conclusion that the learners and tutor agree at the start (i.e. to make £100 profit, or to demonstrate a set standard of work, based on the industry).

Enthusiasm and motivation

All activities and tasks should be delivered in a positive and enthusiastic way – learners pick up on the body and verbal language of their tutors who are, after all, role models. A good way to encourage learners to develop their enthusiasm for a unit is to get them to feel what it is like to teach it to others. Ask learners to develop their peer-teaching skills by preparing and delivering a short practical session (i.e. lunging) having modelled their technique against that of their tutor (or tutors with shared classes).

Tutors can use a 'reflective log' to allow learners to identify the skills that they want to develop in the activity. When setting up the task the tutor should ask learners to draft a short job description for a potential future tutor applying to the college, and they should include a reflection section to evaluate their performance during the activity (they could even evaluate the performance of their tutor, if you are feeling confident). Using video cameras to record the teaching sessions also enables the tutor and the learner to watch themselves back, and develop their reflective practices, as well as building a library of practical sessions for them to track their development over time.

Opportunities for developing confidence and independent learning

As well as running their own businesses tutors can help learners develop confidence and independence by asking learners to organise tasks outside of normal lessons. For example, ask the learners to set up and run a cleaning rota (i.e. for mucking out/grooming) for their peers, or set up a small business, offering their professional services to tutors/peers/public, where appropriate.

The task can be linked to assessment criteria and the wider application of personal, social and industrial skills. The tutor should adapt their support and guidance as the task progresses, and link to course criteria if appropriate, to really contextualise the task for the learners.

High quality resources

Often the most essential resource is overlooked by tutors in practical sessions – namely the horse. There are many ways to integrate the horse into sessions, even theory, which can then be translated into innovative and exciting tasks. One example would be to ask learners to record their equine techniques with their own horses or those from the college or work placement during holidays and breaks, which should be posted to their (or the college's) Moodle pages so that their peers can see what is going on across the class. Using online feedback, the tutor is able to post comments and individual and group feedback online, and the learners' peers are also able to review and support each other's peer learning and reflection.

Opportunities to develop English, maths and functional skills

The development of wider skills can be made simpler with the following task. Ask learners to attend a local event or show (Olympia in December is good as it comes at a festive and fun time of year). Learners should be given a range of industries (or given a specific one) to track during the show (i.e. tack, catering, professional services). Prior to the show, learners could be asked to create a questionnaire based on a related assessment criteria (for example, footfall to stalls, costs of items for sale, comparisons of offers etc.) and use this data in a future assignment, or simply a follow-up task where learners can present their findings and produce a guidebook for potential entrepreneurs wanting to enter that industry.

Tutors can also use guest speakers to visit and share with learners the pitfalls and successes of a range of related topics (i.e. setting up a yard or competing as an amateur/professional) with learners being expected to plan and record the discussions and plan for career and progression ambitions based on session. Finally, tutors should be prepared to identify and track simple grammar and punctuation errors within assignment feedback and set specific targets around these issues.

Integration of Equality and Diversity and Safeguarding

The equine industry carries with it a number of positive (as well as negative) gender and ethnic stereotypes and prejudices, therefore embedding and promoting E&D is easier than tutors might think. For example, ask learners to monitor data collected by the college (or themselves) of those who use the yard during a specific period, or who are represented at shows and events. Learners can then be tasked with drilling down this information based on age, gender, race etc., and complete an assignment that could promote and increase participation for under-represented groups.

(Continued)

(Continued)

For more specific areas, tutors could ask learners to research and trace the history of bloodlines in the equine industry, and comment on the impacts that they might see in horse breeds on their yard. Learners could also consider what would happen if humans did the same!

Activity

Identify three strategies used by Beth and Simon that might translate to your vocational subject.

Case study

Elizabeth is a lecturer in Childcare and Early Years at a private training provider.

I have worked within the sector now for over 15 years. I started out as a nursery nurse and progressed to the role of nursery manager. I have knowledge from both sides of the spectrum, both as a learner and now as a tutor. This has helped me to mentor learners through my working career and I can relate to how they are feeling and also to how hard some learners may find training. My background in childcare started with me completing an NVQ. I find that today, the majority of learners I come across do not believe they can progress to university with these types of qualifications. My own experience with vocational education enables me to change their perceptions and start their thought process that university can be a possibility through a vocational route.

My vocational learners are 14–19 years of age, from all different walks of life. The training setting is within a high deprivation area. A majority of my learners come to the setting with additional issues, such as they are part of the care system. Many learners have been unsuccessful in school and wish to gain qualifications within a college setting.

As we offer a varying selection of courses and we ensure we meet their needs, the learners feel more secure within the setting and this I believe helps them in their learning process. We assist them in any way we can from such things as providing them with bus passes, breakfast. Even something as simple as a bottle of water to drink during lessons can make a great impact on a learner. By showing you are willing to spend the time and effort with them to help them meet their end goal can help motivate and engage learners in more ways than you actually realise.

In my approach to teaching and training, I use a lot of cognitive methods when teaching at the centre. More of the 'behaviourist methods' take place off site whilst on placement, although I believe it is beneficial to have some practical activities within the theoretical lessons to benefit the learners in their ability to engage with the children, i.e. playdough, gloop, flubber and basic baking.

As a manager of a nursery, I have the knowledge of what I would like to see in a learner within my setting. I take this into account when planning lessons as I want the learner to stand out and show both confidence and knowledge within their field. I hope this will then benefit them when it comes to employability. For me, a good learning plan should always consist of a mixture of discussions, activities and research to benefit the learner and ensure learning is taking place. I am fortunate in my role to have classrooms with computers in, which enables me to better meet the needs of all my learners.

We work very closely with the childcare industry and also the health and social care industry too. This helps us ensure our qualifications and teaching methods benefit the client. It also helps in our continuous search for placements and eventually the possibility of employability for our learners.

Within the childcare industry it is hard to arrange trips and visits, but within the health and social care industry we have previously been able to arrange visits to assist care homes in their trips out and visits to local landmarks.

Case study

Hannah is a lecturer in hairdressing at a large FE college

I currently work for a large international company in a busy salon providing a range of hairdressing services to clients. After 18 years in the industry, in various roles, which included managerial, product education and apprenticeship training, I decided to pass on my current skills and knowledge and challenge myself with a change of career direction into teaching.

I began my own hairdressing career with the completion of a National Vocational Qualification (NVQ) at Level 2 through a modern apprenticeship within a salon. Initially I wanted to train within this setting teaching learners much like myself, however my placement for my Certificate in Education course started off within a school teaching 14–16 learners. I then had a second placement working with 16–19-year-old learners within a FE college. Both these experiences changed my perception of vocational education in these types of settings and I found it very rewarding.

I currently teach on a part-time evening programme for adult learners. These particular learners face different challenges within their course. Many choose

(Continued)

(Continued)

to take this mode of study as they have young children and or work during the day, which has the possibility to impact on their attendance. Some of the learners have been out of education for some time and find the study, assignment writing and the use of IT a real challenge. However, all are very keen and very motivated to learn new skills and knowledge in order to change their careers or gain employment within the industry. They all seem to use social networking sites like Facebook and Twitter to keep in touch and to develop as a group when outside of college.

As soon as is possible, my learners are expected to take part in sessions where they provide services for 'real' paying clients. These 'commercial salons' are managed as any salon would be with the delegation of a salon manager on a rota basis. Along with me, learners uphold the code of conduct, decided collectively by the group at the start of the course, and work towards the standards of the industry, including adhering to health and safety.

This is an essential part of the vocational learning programme, in preparing them to be able to work effectively in the industry and to get a job. I encourage and expect the learners to work as part of a team in the setting up, running and closing down of the 'salon'. For example, they need to work together to get the most out of the client services working towards assessments, client care, assisting each other and cleaning duties.

At the start of the session, I expect the learners to use a graphic organiser tool to enable them to reflect on and use their experiences to improve their skills, whether it be actual hairdressing skills, communication and client care or team work. I feel this helps them to develop personal learning and thinking skills (PLTS), which I feel are very important skills to have in the industry if you are to become good at what you do. Hairdressing is an ever-changing profession and you need to have the ability to carry on learning and adapting the skills you have to remain current and creative.

During each practical session, I expect the learners to replicate the roles we would take in industry. They are required to carry out a full consultation before they start a service on a client and relay this information to me, justifying what they are doing and why. This enables me to use questioning to develop and assess their deeper levels of understanding, and as an opportunity to give praise and motivate.

By the nature of the subject, learners tend to have visual and kinaesthetic preferences for learning. To support this, I find getting the learners to physically draw or write (with whiteboard markers) on the mirror the angles, cutting lines, shapes, colour formulations and process they intend to do. This helps me to assess their justification for the approach and helps them to explain, plan clearly and remind themselves what they are doing! Sometimes this allows the learner to question themselves and re-evaluate their course of action. This information can then be transferred to head sheets or the graphic organisers as a memory and reflection aid.

I feel my approach to teaching hairdressing helps to engage and motivate the learners as they can see the relevance of what they are doing and how they can improve and develop as a hairdresser. I have found social media and web tools such as Facebook, YouTube, Twitter and Pinterest (www.pinterest.com) very useful resources when teaching my subject, to engage and motivate the learners. It is invaluable in order for us to communicate and share images that inspire us, or new techniques or equipment. This can then be brought into the workshop environment with the use of the interactive whiteboard where I can demonstrate techniques and tools, or we can 'deconstruct' the methods used to create the 'looks' and learn from them.

At the end of each practical salon session, I involve the learners in group discussion whereby they can share their experiences; for example: what they have learned, what they enjoyed, what assessments/targets they achieved and what they have seen other learners do which they liked or learned from. I feel this works well to help learners support, encourage and praise each other. I also like to share what I believe to be the positives of the session overall as a group, for example effective team work, and to highlight the improvements needed for the next session. These methods are very much 'co-operative' 'learning by doing' and through experience. Although I am there to guide and facilitate, I feel this approach mirrors as closely as possible the real working environment they will experience and the expectations of the learners once in employment.

Activity

Make a list of the ways that Hannah ensures her learning environment is professional, functional and effective. How could you harness the power of learning technologies in your vocational subject?

Case study

Penny is a senior manager in a private international college for creative arts learners

Creative arts has always provoked debate about whether it provides a vocational or an academic experience for learners and what kinds of individuals with what kinds of skills a specialist creative arts education produces.

It is probably possible to argue that the study of creative arts sits between a vocational and an academic experience and combines both to provide an education (learning experience) which includes recognised best practice in teaching, learning and assessment. Leonardo da Vinci is often cited as an example of someone who uses skills from different subject domains to create, invent and make.

(Continued)

(Continued)

At my private college post-16 international learners simultaneously take two Level 3 qualifications provided by two different organisations. My learners have very different backgrounds and are used to very different methods of teaching in previous schools and countries. They find team work, independent learning and working through a creative process challenging. They are comfortable with technical skill development and completing tasks.

The Foundation Diploma and A levels can cover similar ground as there is flexibility in the way they can be delivered but achievement is evidenced and assessed differently. Progression to university-level education is based on learners' portfolios which demonstrate their skills application.

To ensure learners have as rich a programme as possible, it is important to provide a flexible and well-resourced experience:

- *The private school is boarding and the art studios are open and supervised by staff all evening and at weekends. Learners spend a long time working because they enjoy their work and they enjoy the studio atmosphere. Time in learning.*

- *There is a great deal of planned stimulation from staff, practising artists, graduates, exhibitions, workshops, academic visits. Motivation, aim and context.*

- *Learners take several arts subjects and become technically competent in several areas. High skills level application.*

- *Learners discuss work with each other and staff for longer periods. They seize opportunities. Confidence and resourcefulness.*

- *Learners spend a long time on primary/secondary research, developing ideas and experimenting/refining in context. Conceptual grounding.*

- *Learners develop individual identity through chosen pathways. Specialisation, individuality and understanding.*

Activity

Can you identify any approaches that Penny's college takes that would enhance your own vocational study programme? What would you need to do to implement your identified intervention?

Activity

Final activity

Now that you have come to the end of the book, we would like you to take some time to reflect on the content and how it might impact on your practice as an excellent vocational tutor

Theme	Reflections, actions, next steps
What is vocational education?	
The current landscape	
Engaging and motivating vocational learners	
Employer engagement	
Planning your approach	
Experiential and applied learning	

(Continued)

(Continued)

Vocational assessment	
Recording vocational assessment evidence	

Now reflect on and devise a CPD plan to strengthen how you plan to:

- *create a welcoming, supportive classroom, workshop, salon that is inclusive of all cultures, genders, special needs, interests and capabilities;*

- *integrate learning within contexts of real-life situations, investigations, routines and transitions, and focused learning and teaching;*

- *consider the problematic nature of inquiry-based learning to acquire deep knowledge;*

- *encourage collaborative learning approaches in each context for learning;*

- *include learners' diverse backgrounds, e.g. social, cultural, lifestyle, familial setting, prior education/care contexts as a focus for vocational curriculum decision-making;*

- *provide real-life learning that reflects and responds to community needs/ interests;*

- *provide equitable access to resources, storage and furniture for all learners;*

- *develop and promote an approach which focuses on the process of learning and encourages learners to adopt a 'growth mindset' to their own development;*

- *raise the profile of high quality, effective and life-transforming vocational education and training.*

Reading and reflecting on, issues in education can help our classroom practice, stimulate our imaginations and enhance our professionalism. And it can take you in unexpected directions…

Good luck in your future career.

APPENDIX I   EXAMPLE OF A VOCATIONAL SCHEME OF WORK

Course programme: BTEC L3 Diploma in Health & Social Care Module: Unit 34 – Human Inheritance for Health & Social Care

Session number	Learning objectives and content linked to the syllabus	Teaching strategies and learner activity	Materials/resources/ learning technologies	Opportunities to embed functional skills	Opportunities to address wider skills development	Assessment internal/ external
I Intro to Unit 34	Module breakdown Module introduction Overview of assignments to be given **Learning objective –** **Understand human reproduction** Review human reproduction ***	Verbal questioning of learners' knowledge of what they already know about human reproduction. Some simple terms they should be familiar with. Presented on PowerPoint which learners should complete in their own words in their learner glossary worksheet/booklets. ***	Simple diagrams of reproductive systems that learners can annotate as tutor runs though the main points of the PowerPoint. Colouring pages of fertilisation, conception to embryo and initial embryonic development. *** Chromosome structure and function workbooks. Online video ref cell growth.	Filling in glossary worksheet/booklet allows embedding of key technical terms and fulfils learner language acquisition. Completing colouring activity will enforce key terms and allow concepts to be visualised by learner. The use of online videos and tutorials will familiarise the learner with ICT.	The use of dictionaries (glossaries) and images that the learner has to annotate or improve will help to optimise the learning experience. This is enforced by the use of learner-centred discussions allowing time for each learner to voice their opinions and feel confident and valued in class and understand that they are in a safe (non-conflict) environment.	Internally and externally moderated assignments (4 in total) ***

(Continued)

Appendix I **(Continued)**

Session number	Learning objectives and content linked to the syllabus	Teaching strategies and learner activity	Materials/resources/ learning technologies	Opportunities to embed functional skills	Opportunities to address wider skills development	Assessment internal/ external
	Introduction to chromosome structure Mitosis and meiosis	Workbooks based on chromosome structure and function and outline of stages in cell growth and cellular reproduction – learners to annotate workbooks fully. Tutor will talk through online video highlighting key points and advise learners to look at these in their own time and attempt the questions on the site to expand their knowledge and prepare for the next session.		Direct learners to college LRC if they do not have internet access at home. The tutor should also reinforce the fact that the learner MUST use reputable sources for knowledge. Effective participators/ reflective learners – learners will be able to help each other complete tasks and refer back to previous subject knowledge. Independent enquirers- learners will be offered extension activities and access to higher-level materials by referring to further reading in workbooks.	The use of workbooks will allow the learners to develop an enquiring attitude and the use of further references will direct them where they may find further information to do their own research Allowing learners to use the internet as a potential source of information will encourage and highlight safe use of the world wide web and allow learners to pursue their goals in an engaging way.	Internal assessment – responses to questioning and completion of worksheets allows tutor to determine the initial level of the learners and will determine gaps in knowledge and thus set the pace of the session.

Appendix I (Continued)

Session number	Learning objectives and content linked to the syllabus	Teaching strategies and learner activity	Materials/resources/learning technologies	Opportunities to embed functional skills	Opportunities to address wider skills development	Assessment internal/external
2 Gametogenesis	Learning objectives – Gametogenesis Genetic codes Structure of DNA Recap on chromosome structure Meiosis and mitosis in detail Introduce Assignment I of 4	Quick-fire open questions on key terms/concepts from last session. Activity – domino or matching cards on key terms and definitions in groups of three maximum. Allow learners time to write down definitions if needed. Tutor to run through terms on PowerPoint. Recap on previous session, asking and answering questions from learners. When sure learners are familiar and happy with key definitions continue on to learning objectives.	PowerPoint with key terms/concepts arranged on it. Use online video clips: comparison of meiosis and mitosis and stages of meiosis. Domino/matching cards meiosis/mitosis. Assignment I – learners to produce a model of DNA and chromosomes showing understanding of structure and function (in own time activity). Learners to produce a poster showing meiosis stages in detail and sex determination – in class activity – groups of two or three.	Numeracy is embedded as learners will identify chromosome numbers and complete comparisons of diploid and haploid. Reduction and combination of gametes. Effective participators/team workers – learners will support each other and work in groups to complete tasks. Creative thinkers – the assignment is a visual one. Learners will need to express their opinions and present their work in a creative format.	Learners will work in groups they are familiar/confident with. They will choose their own partners allowing peer assessment, enjoyment and achievement. Each will make a positive contribution to the group work and successful achievement of this assessment will promote learner health and wellbeing The working environment fulfils all Maslow's hierarchy of needs – warm, comfortable and appropriate to learning.	Internal – check learner glossaries are correct and progressing. Identify level/gaps in knowledge. Official Assignment I learners are to start work on a poster which they will present to tutors and rest of class.

(Continued)

Appendix I   (Continued)

Session number	Learning objectives and content linked to the syllabus	Teaching strategies and learner activity	Materials/resources/ learning technologies	Opportunities to embed functional skills	Opportunities to address wider skills development	Assessment internal/ external
		Run through binding of nucleotides asking learners to show how DNA pairs

mitosis – cell growth – diploid

meiosis – gamete production – reduction of chromosomes.

Learners to make notes and watch videos on meiosis and mitosis. Make a start on Assignment I.

Read through assignment brief – clarifying any issues. | Poster paper, coloured pens, pencils, glue sticks, computer use, printer paper.

Genetics textbook and flashcards. Hand out Assignment I – brief and run through ensuring understanding. | Self-managers – although working in groups learners must assign tasks to be completed by each individual. | | Poster content will be marked and submitted for IV/portfolio and presentation will be marked by tutor observation. |

Appendix 1 (Continued)

Session number	Learning objectives and content linked to the syllabus	Teaching strategies and learner activity	Materials/resources/learning technologies	Opportunities to embed functional skills	Opportunities to address wider skills development	Assessment internal/external
3 Genetic coding and protein synthesis	Learning objectives – Understand relationship between genetic codes and protein production and chromosomal structure	Recap on meiosis – use flashcards and pictures of onion cell. Activity – learners to arrange pictures in correct order from prophase to cytokinesis.	PowerPoint on protein synthesis. Meiosis flashcards. Onion cell pictures.	Use of ICT, technical terms and creative activities allowing learner knowledge acquisition.	Hands-on activities showing creativity and planning (positive contributions). VAK styles incorporated (enjoy and achieve).	Completion of cards and pictures shows understanding of stages of cell growth and repair.
	Recap on DNA pairing, introduce protein synthesis – transcription, translation.	PowerPoint protein synthesis from DNA-RNA-proteins. Use worksheet on protein synthesis and learners to add notes whilst listening and asking questions if clarification required.	Protein synthesis worksheets. Chromosome sets showing sizes of chromosomes. Welcome Trust from DNA to protein animations – on memory stick.	Effective participators/team workers – learners will support each other and work in groups to complete tasks.	Development of skills (economic wellbeing). Healthy working environment including breaks. Promotion of respectful environment so no question is a silly question.	Correct completion of DNA-protein translation identifies some key genes present on chromosomes.
	Identify genes on chromosomes and understand that chromosome size varies.	Activity – what does this DNA sequence code for? Identifies how researchers can understand how chromosomes code for and express genes. Learners to research human genome project for homework to meet assignment criteria.	DNA coding activity sheets and wheels.			

(Continued)

Appendix I (Continued)

Session number	Learning objectives and content linked to the syllabus	Teaching strategies and learner activity	Materials/resources/ learning technologies	Opportunities to embed functional skills	Opportunities to address wider skills development	Assessment internal/ external
4 Part I – Learner presentation Part 2 – Influences on reproduction	Learning objectives – Understand factors/ influences on reproduction Diet/health/age etc. Down's syndrome non disjunction.	Learners to present posters/models to peers. Tutors will reassure, note observations and ask questions (if needed) to ensure all criteria fulfilled. Remind class to show respect by listening to each other. *** Activity – order human chromosomes and decide what is missing or extra. How do we write genetic notation?	Whiteboard, blue tack for poster presentations. Observation sheets. Criteria for Assignment I, camera for portfolio photographs. Chocolates for reward/ icebreaker. *** Human genome set of chromosomes in envelopes.	Learners will be encouraged to speak and present their work clearly, others will be reminded that everyone should respect others' time and contribute by showing attention. Learners will be marked on their creativity and participation as well as content and accuracy.	Achievement and enjoyment – successful completion of this session will give learners credit towards their final grade. Learners must be reminded to work together with mutual respect and in a safe and comfortable environment.	Assessment I – internal but may be verified by external (requires presence of second tutor to sign off observation worksheets ensuring fairness and validity).

Appendix I (Continued)

Session number	Learning objectives and content linked to the syllabus	Teaching strategies and learner activity	Materials/resources/ learning technologies	Opportunities to embed functional skills	Opportunities to address wider skills development	Assessment internal/ external
		Learners to make notes, watch video, perform karyotyping online activity. Internet video where meiosis goes wrong – non-disjunction. PowerPoint and worksheets. Case study: Down's Syndrome.	Show video clip: Where meiosis goes wrong. Karyotyping activity links: http://www.biology. arizona.edu/human_bio/ activities/karyotyping/ karyotyping.html Case study: Down's Syndrome.	Use of ICT as a fulfilment for assignment criteria and use of Turnitin website as a marking/plagiarism tool.	Displays of learner work and input shows that learners have made a valid and positive contribution to the class and developed skills they can use in the wider community.	Completion of Karyotyping activity fulfils part of Assignment 2.

(Continued)

Appendix1 (Continued)

Session number	Learning objectives and content linked to the syllabus	Teaching strategies and learner activity	Materials/resources/ learning technologies	Opportunities to embed functional skills	Opportunities to address wider skills development	Assessment internal/ external
5 **Assignment 2 – Influences and impact on reproduction**	**Learning objective –** **Investigate the impact on individuals due to genetic abnormalities** Recap on factors affecting reproduction. Look at PIES for patients/ families/society due to failure of reproductive process.	Recap on meiosis going wrong – genetic notations. PowerPoint identifying resources for assignment, factors affecting reproduction and physical, intellectual, emotional and spiritual needs for affected individuals. Class discussion on factors (recap and relate to Unit 14 which they have completed). Learners to identify and research a genetic disorder based on chromosomal abnormalities. Given list to choose from. Use ICT and library resources to help.	Assignment 2: brief. PowerPoint. Assignment resources sheet – list of useful websites/books/ periodicals. List of acceptable disorders for learners to research. Keywords from Unit 14 – care plans link to this unit.	Learners should compare their keywords from Unit 14 and recap them for this assignment. Embed Health and Social Care vocabulary. ICT use of internet to research syndrome. Effective participators/ reflective learners – learners will need to participate in discussion and reflect back to previous knowledge from modules completed. Independent enquirers – learners will discuss matters and listen to others' points of view.	This assignment will promote learners understanding of health and wellbeing, allowing a positive contribution to their environment and community by discussing disorders and how other people envision them.	Internal – participation in the discussion will identify ways in which the learner can successfully complete their formal assignment. Assignment 2 will form part of portfolio/final grade.

Appendix I (Continued)

Session number	Learning objectives and content linked to the syllabus	Teaching strategies and learner activity	Materials/resources/ learning technologies	Opportunities to embed functional skills	Opportunities to address wider skills development	Assessment internal/ external
6 Assignment 3 – Mendelian genetics	**Learning objective – Identify key principles of genetics** Investigate Mendel the father of genetics using key examples – peas, flower colour Identification of traits/genes (dominant and recessive genes). Mendel's laws – inheritance and variation. Punnett squares. Carry out monohybrid, test and dihybrid crosses. Mendel's Ratios.	Recap – check learners are on task for Assignment 2 and answer any outstanding queries before moving on to Mendel. PowerPoint on the life of Gregor Mendel – who he was and why he is important. Hand out glossary sheet of genetic terms. Activity – Punnett Square worksheets for flower colour and pea shape/ colour. Mendel workbooks. Online activity – Virtual Peas.	PowerPoint. Glossary of terms key cards for learners to pass around. Mendel workbooks. Virtual laboratory online activity where key words are explained and Punnett Square activities can be completed: http://www.ngfl-cymru.org. uk/VTC/2012-13/biology/ echalk/genes-and-variety/ eng/startHere.html	Numeracy is embedded here as learners will be working out ratios to determine inheritance. Learners will need to be steeped in correct terminology enabling determination of genotype and phenotype ratios. Independent enquirers – there is a lot of information on this task website which learners can use to explore and extend their knowledge.	ICT and language embedding will empower learners and the use of visual, stimulating online activities encourages learner independence and allows for different learning styles and habits.	Internal correct crosses by online activities printed out and added to workbooks for marking. Formal – completed workbooks will comprise large portion of Assignment 3.

(Continued)

Appendix 1 (Continued)

Session number	Learning objectives and content linked to the syllabus	Teaching strategies and learner activity	Materials/resources/ learning technologies	Opportunities to embed functional skills	Opportunities to address wider skills development	Assessment internal/ external
7 Mendelian genetics	**Learning objective –** **Human inheritance and key principles of genetics** Continue with test crosses and work on dihybrid crosses, more complex Punnett Squares. Continuous and discontinuous variation.	Recap on Punnett Squares and genetic crosses. PowerPoint Mendel workbooks. Activity – virtual fruit fly laboratory online work.	Variety of differentiated worksheets for genetic crosses related to human inheritance and variation. http://www. sciencecourseware. org/vcise/drosophila/ Drosophila. php?guestaccess=1 Learners to research sickle cell for next week.	Numeracy is embedded here as learners will be working out ratios to determine inheritance. Learners will need to be steeped in correct terminology enabling determination of genotype and phenotype ratios.	ICT and language embedding will empower learners and the use of visual, stimulating online activities encourages learner independence and allows for different learning styles and habits.	Internal correct crosses by online activities printed out and added to workbooks for marking. Formal – completed workbooks will comprise large portion of Assignment 3.

Session number	Learning objectives and content linked to the syllabus	Teaching strategies and learner activity	Materials/resources/ learning technologies	Opportunities to embed functional skills	Opportunities to address wider skills development	Assessment internal/ external
8 Mendelian genetics	**Learning objective –** **Human inheritance and key principles of genetics** Look at Mendel and how it relates to human inheritance, e.g. cystic fibrosis, Huntington's disease and sickle cell anaemia.	PowerPoint. Workbooks. Learners to research sickle cell for part of Assignment 3. Recap on subject so far, deeper look at genetic disorders such as cystic fibrosis and Huntington's Give assignment brief for Merit of Assignment 3 – sickle cell.	Assignment brief for Merit of assignment 3 – sickle cell. Worksheets on family trees and inheritance. Computers for learner research on sickle cell.	Learners will be bringing everything together for their third assignment so all numeracy, literacy and ICT skills gained so far will be used to complete Assignment 3.	Successful completion of assignment will enable learners to achieve.	Internal/external Hand in of Assignment 3, which will form part of final portfolio.

(Continued)

Appendix 1 (Continued)

Session number	Learning objectives and content linked to the syllabus	Teaching strategies and learner activity	Materials/resources/learning technologies	Opportunities to embed functional skills	Opportunities to address wider skills development	Assessment internal/external
9

Assignment 4 – Reproduction and technology | **Learning objective – Reproductive gene technologies**

Introduction to genetic counselling, in vitro fertilisation (IVF), stem cells and gene therapy.

Ethical dilemmas. | PowerPoint presentation and class discussion.

Use of case studies and vocational scenario worksheets.

Learner-centred activity tutor will ask questions. Learners will hold voting cards and elaborate as necessary.

Learners will pass ball amongst each other to discuss ethical scenarios from everyday life.

Learners may work in groups for second part of session then present their findings/arguments to the rest of the class.

Tutor will referee and observe, ensuring learners are considerate of others' views. | Ball to use as speaking object.

Lists of questions.

Disagree/agree cards.

Case scenarios.

Interactive whiteboard.

Learner observation sheets. | Speaking and listening and debating skills.

Team work, independent thinking and creative enquiry – learners will set and push their own boundaries and be challenged in their thoughts and emotions.

Reflection is important as they will need to identify implications and expand upon them.

Effective participators – learners must put across their points to achieve a distinction in this assignment and use this knowledge in next week's visit to the university. | Learners will have strong opinions here and it is essential that they do not attack each other if views are different. The tutors should ensure that learners feel able to contribute in any way without fear of recrimination.

The learners' participation will allow them to achieve marks towards their final assignment grade (Assignment 4), fulfilling, enjoy and achieve, positive contribution and economic wellbeing (will help towards grades to move on to future courses/increase employability).

Scenarios are based around real health and social care issues encouraging future health and wellbeing of learners/colleagues and patients. | Assignment 4 observation sheets into final portfolio (requires presence of second tutor to sign off observation worksheets ensuring fairness and validity). |

Session number	Learning objectives and content linked to the syllabus	Teaching strategies and learner activity	Materials/resources/ learning technologies	Opportunities to embed functional skills	Opportunities to address wider skills development	Assessment internal/ external
10 Ethics and gene technologies	Learning objective – Reproductive gene technologies Visit to university for 'a breath of fresh air' debate.	Trip to university. Need to complete risk assessment and sign in learner record sheets for university. Emergency contact details to college in case of emergency or unforeseen issues.	Risk assessment sheets. Learner sign in sheets and contact details. Learner observation sheets. University will provide all resources.	Opportunity to work together in collaborative groups, asking questions and communicating clearly to academics and learners from other institutions.	Raising aspirations through expose to higher-level study and a HE environment. Opportunities to develop knowledge of HE finance and HE life.	Assignment 4 observation sheets into final portfolio.
11 Review and sign off	Unit review Check any outstanding assignments are completed. Tutorials 1-2-1 if required.	Learner Professional Development Portfolios (PDP). Update learner outcomes, PDPs and allow time to work through action plans. Review and record assessment strategies with learners. Allow time for completing/resubmitting outstanding work.	e-Portfolios Learning resource centre. Final submission paperwork.	Focus on accuracy of written evidence – applied English language skills.	Enjoy and achieve.	

(Continued)

Appendix 1 (Continued)

Session number	Learning objectives and content linked to the syllabus	Teaching strategies and learner activity	Materials/resources/learning technologies	Opportunities to embed functional skills	Opportunities to address wider skills development	Assessment internal/external
12 **Review and sign off**	**Tutorials and Learner feedback on module** Sign off learner work for portfolio ready for Internal and External Verification.	Learner Professional Development Portfolios (PDP). Complete evaluation questionnaires. Update learner outcomes, PDPs and allow time to work through action plans. Review and record assessment strategies with learners. Allow time for completing/resubmitting outstanding work.	ePortfolios Learning resource centre Final submission paperwork	Focus on accuracy of written evidence – applied English language skills.	Enjoy and achieve.	

APPENDIX 2   ASSESSMENT PLAN TEMPLATE

Assessment Plan

Qualification/Course:

Programme Leader:

Unit Number and Title	Assignment	Outcomes	Assessment Criteria	Issue Date	Interim Feedback Date	Submission Deadline	Final Assessment Date	IV Sampling Date	Resubmission Date	Assessor Name	IV Name
Year 1											
Year 2											

| Programme Leader Signature | Name | | | | | | | Date | |
| Internal Verifier (IV) Signature | Name | | | | | | | Date | |

APPENDIX 3 IRIS REFLECTION TEMPLATE

IRIS: Independent Reflective Investigation for Solution(s)

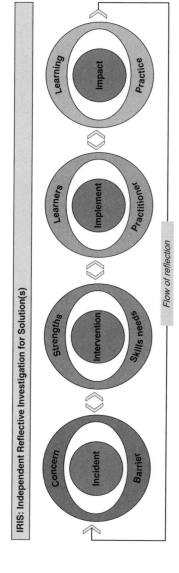

Flow of reflection

Identify a particular critical incident. Describe the incident—what is, or are your concerns? Have you identified a barrier to success?	Having identified an incidence of your practice, consider an intervention(s) that might address your concerns. How can this intervention build on your existing strengths? What skills might you need to develop and who could support you through move through the flow?	Having identified a possible intervention, how might you practically implement this? What could you do to make it happen?	Now consider what impact the intervention might have. What would a success look like? Are there any areas of risk? How will you measure the impact? Was the implementation successful? Do you have any further concerns?

Adapted from: Ingle S and Duckworth V (2013) *Enhancing Learning through Technology in Lifelong Learning: Fresh Ideas; Innovative Strategies*. Maidenhead: Open University Press.

INDEX

'academic' 4
activists 84
adult learners, characteristics of 21
Adult Learners' Week 117
Advanced Learning Loans 30
andragogy 21
anti-discriminatory approaches 48
Applied A levels 10
Applied GCSEs 10
applied learning 103
apprenticeships 7–8, 28–9
assessment 66, 125–39
   approaches 126
   effective 131
   planning 139, 179
   tools 128, 138
   types 129–30
assignment brief 135–7
Association of Colleges (AoC) 39
Association of Employment and Learning Providers
   (AELP) 35
attribution theory 55

Baker Dearing Educational Trust 5
behaviourism 43
blended learning 32
Broadsheet 34
Bookfield, S 114
Brooks, S 51
BTEC qualifications xi
bursary fund 30
Business in the Community (BITC) 37
business-like attitudes 19

case studies 14, 33, 61, 66, 68, 69, 77, 92, 107–9,
   111–13, 119–20, 132, 137–8, 152–62
Centre for Skills Development (CSD) 38
changes xi, 24–39
   contexts 31–3
   costs 30
   policy 25–9
Chartered Institute of Educational Assessors 36
CHIME xii, 41–2
City and Guilds Centre for Skills Development 80
coaching 110–13
Coffield, F 83, 84
cognitivism 43

Commission for UK Employment and Skills
   (UKCES) xv
Commission on Adult Vocational Teaching and
   Learning (CAVTL) 2–3, 18, 60
*Common Inspection Framework for Learning and
   Skills* 152
competition 56, 115–17
confidence 50
contexts 31–3
continual professional development 15, 16
co-operative teaching and learning 121
   planning 122
costs 30
course design 64–5
craftsmanship 19, 20
CREATE skills framework 31
criterion referenced assessment 130
critical lenses for reflection 114
Csikszentmihalyi, M 53

Deci, E 58
Department for Business, Skills and Innovation
   (BIS) 37
Department for Education 27, 60
Dewey, J 103, 113
diagnostic assessment 129
differentiate learning 54
digital literacies 92
distance learning 32
dual professionalism 16, 151
Duckworth, V 51, 88
Dweck, C 52, 85

Edexcel Policy Watch 34
Edge Foundation 3, 5, 34, 117
Education and Training Foundation 29, 35
Education Business Partnerships (EBPs) 35
Education Funding Agency (EDA) 37
e-learning 32
employer engagement 59–72
employer panel 65
enterprise academies 32
enterprise education 60
enterprise projects 60
e-portfolios 92, 142
Equality Act 2010 45
ethics 147

European Prison Education Association
(EPEA) 38
evidence 141–3
authentic 143
and ethics 147
recording 145
reliable 143
expectancy value theory 54–5
experience 21
experiential learning 103–4
extrinsic motivators 50–1

Facebook 67
FE and skills organisations 35–9
FE News 34
FE Week 34
Federation for Industry Sector Skills and
Standards 35
Federation of Awarding Bodies 37
feedback 66, 132–4
Fishbein, M 54
flipped classroom approach 107
formative assessment 129
functional literacies 19, 20
functional skills 90–1
Further Education Reputation Strategy Group
(FERSG) 38
FutureLab 118

Gagne, R 81
games 118
Gibbs, G 113
group profile 78
GROW model 110
growth mindset 52, 85
through feedback 133

*Handbook for the Inspection of Further Education and
Skills* 47
health and safety 79
Health and Safety Executive 45
Heider, F 55
Holex 38
Honey, P 84
humanistic 43

ipsative assessment 130
Independent Reflective Investigation for Solution(s)
model (IRIS) 114, 180
initial teacher training (ITT) 29
Innovation in Vocational Education and Training 34
Institute for Learning (IfL) 15, 26, 36
intrinsic motivation 51
Investing in Skills for Sustainable Growth 25

jargon 88, 90
Joint Council for Qualifications 144
Joint Information Systems Committee (JISC) 32
Jones, P 32
Journal of Vocational Education and Training 34

Knowles, M 21
Kolb, D 104, 113

Land Based College Aspiring To Excellence
(Landex) 38
language 46
LEAP model 110
learner types 47
learners' literacies 87
Learning and Skills Improvement Service
(LSIS) 56
Learning and Skills Network 80
learning log 145
learning outside the classroom 65
Learning Records Service (LRS) 37
learning styles 83–5
learning through competing 115–18
learning through playing games 118–21
learning through practice 105
learning through reflection 113–15
learning through virtual learning environments 106
Lifelong Learning UK (LLUK) xiv
Lingfield Review of professionalism in further
education xi, 29
LinkedIn 67
Local Enterprise Partnerships (LEPs) 35
Lucas, B 10, 19, 22, 105

maintaining currency 34
malpractice 144
Maslow, AH 44
meaningful work experience 27
meeting individual needs 44–8
mentoring 60
mindset 52–5, 75, 85–7, 133
motivation to learn 21, 42–4
lack of 55–6
promoting 56–7
theories of 44
through competition 56
Mumford, A 84

National Apprenticeship Service (NAS) 36, 117
National Apprenticeship Week 117
National Careers Service (NCS) 38
National Institute of Adult Continuing Education
(NIACE) 38, 117
National Occupational Standards (NOS) xiv
National Training Federation Wales (NTfW) 39
National Vocational Qualifications (NVQs) 9, 13
New Challenges, New Chances 25
New Literacy Studies 87

observation records 146
observing vocational learning 141–50
Office for Qualifications and Examination
Regulation (Ofqual) 36
Office for Standards in Education (Ofsted) 11, 37
optimal challenge 53
orientation to learning 21

PAR model of teaching 81
pedagogy 18
personal development records (PDR) 142
personal learning and thinking skills (PLTS) 63
Personally Accountable Learning (PAL) 33
Petty, G 80
Pinterest 67
plagiarism 144
planning 74–101
   key considerations 75
   paperwork 76
policy 25–9
portfolios 142
practitioner voice 151
pragmatists 85
problem-based learning (PBL) 105
professional standards 1, 24, 41, 59, 74, 103,
   125, 141, 151
professionalism in further education 29

qualifications comparison 13–14
Qualified Teacher Learning Status (QTLS) 26, 29
questioning 134

readiness to learn 21
real-world problem-solving 105
recognising and recording progress and achievement
   (RARPA) 6, 81–2
   initial and diagnostic 82
recording practical skills 145
reflection cycle 113
reflectors 84
resourcefulness 19
Richard Review of Apprenticeships xi, 28–9
Richardson, W 5
risk assessments 45
role models 61
routine expertise 19, 20

scheme of work (SOW) 76, 165–78
Schön, DA 113
Sector Skills Council (SSC) xiv
sector skills organisations 16–18, 36
sector subject areas (SSA) 11
self-concept 21
self-determination theory 52
self-esteem 50
session plan 77–8, 93–101
situated learning 43
Sixth Form Colleges' Association (SFCA) 38
Skills for Sustainable Growth 25
Skills Funding Agency (SFA) 37

social media 67
stereotypes 48–50
studio schools xi, 31
summative assessment 130

Teaching and Learning Research Programme 87
teaching models 80–1
Technical Baccalaureate (TechBacc) 10
terminology 88–90
theorists 85
Third Sector National Learning Alliance (TSNLA) 38
Times Education Supplement 34
Tolhurst, J 110
traineeships 8–9
training 3
Training Assessment quality Assurance (TAQA) xiv
Tummons, J 2
Twitter 67

UK Commission for Employment and Skills 36, 42
University Technical Colleges (UTCs) xi, 31

VARK model 83
virtual learning environments (VLE) 92, 106
vocational andragogy 21
vocational assessment 125–39
vocational education
   distinction from 'academic' 4
   what is 1–2
vocational literacies 88
vocational pedagogy 18–20, 76
vocational qualifications 6–18, 26, 28
vocational role models 61
vocational work experience 27
Vocationally Related Qualifications (VRQs) 4, 10
VQ Day 117

Whitmore, J 110
Wiborg, S 5
wider skills for growth 19, 20
witness testimonies 146
Wolf, A 5, 25
Wolf Review of Vocational Education xi, 2, 5–6, 25, 126
work placement 62
work-related qualifications 9
work shadowing 60
working competence 19
workshops 60
World Skills International 115
World Skills UK 56, 115

YouTube 67